Flexibility in School Programs

THE NATIONAL SOCIETY FOR THE STUDY OF EDUCATION

Series on Contemporary Educational Issues
Kenneth J. Rehage, Series Editor

The 1971 Titles

Accountability in Education, Leon M. Lessinger and Ralph W. Tyler, Editors
Farewell to Schools??? Daniel U. Levine and Robert J. Havighurst, Editors
Models for Integrated Education, Daniel U. Levine, Editor
PYGMALION Reconsidered, Janet D. Elashoff and Richard E. Snow
Reactions to Silberman's CRISIS IN THE CLASSROOM, A. Harry Passow, Editor

The 1972 Titles

Black Students in White Schools, Edgar A. Epps, Editor
Flexibility in School Programs, Willard J. Congreve and George J. Rinehart, Editors
Performance Contracting—1969-1971, James A. Mecklenburger
The Potential of Educational Futures, Michael Marien and Warren L. Ziegler, Editors
Sex Differences and Discrimination in Education, Scarvia Anderson, Editor

The National Society for the Study of Education also publishes Yearbooks which are distributed by the University of Chicago Press.

Inquiries regarding membership in the Society may be addressed to Kenneth J. Rehage, Secretary-Treasurer, 5835 Kimbark Avenue, Chicago 60637.

Flexibility in School Programs

edited by

Willard J. Congreve
Washington Township Public School District,
Sewell, New Jersey

and

George J. Rinehart
Eldora (Iowa) Community Schools

Charles A. Jones Publishing Company
Worthington, Ohio

Contributors

Willard J. Congreve, superintendent, Washington Township Public School District, Sewell, New Jersey

David L. Cronin, director, School Without Walls, Newton (Iowa) Public Schools

Ronald L. DeWitt, director, Project CREATES, Tucson (Arizona) Public Schools

Don Glines, director, the Wilson School and the School of Educational Alternatives, Mankato State College, Mankato, Minnesota

Marv Harmon, assistant principal, Hood River (Oregon) Valley High School

Catherine Johnson, guidance director, Ninety Six (South Carolina) High School

Kenneth R. Kimball, Jr., principal, Farnsworth Middle School, Guilderland, New York

James D. Rangles, research counsellor, Ontario (California) High School

George J. Rinehart, Eldora (Iowa) Community Schools

Robert J. Ross, principal, Paul A. Smith School, Franklin, New Hampshire

Wilbur R. Smith, principal, Woodrow Wilson Elementary School, Newton (Iowa) Public Schools

2 3 4 5 6 7 8 9 10 / 76 75 74 73

Library of Congress Catalog Card Number: 72-85890
International Standard Book Number: 0-8396-0025-9

Printed in the United States of America

Series Foreword

Flexibility in School Programs is one of a group of five publications constituting the second set in a series prepared under the auspices of the National Society for the Study of Education. Other titles in this second set of paperbacks dealing with "Contemporary Educational Issues" are:

Performance Contracting—1969-1971, by James Mecklenburger

Sex Differences and Discrimination in Education, edited by Scarvia B. Anderson

Black Students in White Schools, edited by Edgar G. Epps

The Potential of Educational Futures, edited by Michael Marien and Warren L. Ziegler

The response to the first set of five paperbacks in this series, published in 1971, has been very encouraging. Like their predecessors the current volumes, all dealing with timely and significant issues in education, present a useful background and analysis for those who seek a deeper understanding of some of the critical educational problems of our times.

In this volume Willard J. Congreve and George J. Rinehart, both leaders in public schools, describe the results of a nationwide inquiry in which they sought to determine what schools are now doing in order to achieve flexibility in educational programs. In addition to their own descriptions and analyses they have included invited essays from eight school systems across the country. The contributors were asked to report both successes and difficulties encountered in moving toward more flexible programs. The result is a collection of reports providing stimulating ideas for those who likewise search for practices that will make schools truly responsive to the needs of today's youth.

The Society wishes to acknowledge its appreciation to Messrs. Congreve and Rinehart, and to the various contributors to this volume, for their work in bringing together this important collection of essays. We also wish to acknowledge the assistance of the many educators across the country who provided the editors with information essential to the completion of this effort.

Kenneth J. Rehage
for the Committee on the Expanded Publication
Program of the National Society for the Study of Education

The Charles A. Jones Publishing Company

International Series in Education

Adams, *Simulation Games*
Allen, Barnes, Reece, Roberson, *Teacher Self-Appraisal: A Way of Looking Over Your Own Shoulder*
Armstrong, Cornell, Kraner, Roberson, *The Development and Evaluation of Behavioral Objectives*
Braun, Edwards, *History and Theory of Early Childhood Education*
Carlton, Goodwin, *The Collective Dilemma: Negotiations in Education*
Criscuolo, *Improving Classroom Reading Instruction*
Crosswhite, Higgins, Osborne, Shumway, *Mathematics Teaching: Psychological Foundations*
Denues, *Career Perspective: Your Choice of Work*
DeStefano, *Language, Society, and Education: A Profile of Black English*
Doll, *Leadership to Improve Schools*
Drier, *K-12 Guide for Integrating Career Development into Local Curriculum*
Foster, Fitzgerald, Beal, *Career Education and Vocational Guidance*
Frymier, Hawn, *Curriculum Improvement for Better Schools*
Goodlad, Klein, Associates, *Behind the Classroom Door*
Hauenstein, *Curriculum Planning for Behavioral Development*
Higgins, *Mathematics Teaching and Learning*
Hitt, *Education as a Human Enterprise*
Leland, Smith, *Mental Retardation: Perspectives for the Future*
Lutz, *Toward Improved Urban Education*
Meyer, *A Statistical Analysis of Behavior*
National Society for the Study of Education, *Contemporary Educational Issues* (10 book series)
Nerbovig, *Unit Planning: A Model for Curriculum Development*
Overly, Kinghorn, Preston, *The Middle School: Humanizing Education for Youth*
Perry, Wildman, *The Impact of Negotiations in Public Education: The Evidence from the Schools*
Poston, *Implementing Career Education*
Pula, Goff, *Technology in Education: Challenge and Change*
Ressler, *Career Education: The New Frontier*
Rich, *Humanistic Foundations of Education*
Shane, Shane, Gibson, Munger, *Guiding Human Development: The Counselor and the Teacher in the Elementary School*
Swanson, *Evaluation in Education*
Thiagarajan, *The Programing Process: A Practical Guide*
Von Haden, King, *Innovations in Education: Their Pros and Cons*
Weber, *Early Childhood Education: Perspectives on Change*
Wernick, *Career Education in the Elementary School*
Wiles, *Changing Perspectives in Educational Research*
Wiman, *Instructional Materials*

Preface

This book is primarily for the practicing educator. It has been born out of practice. It focuses directly on the questions: What procedures are schools using to achieve flexibility? To what extent do they enable the schools to attain learning objectives heretofore not realized?

In attempting to identify procedures to achieve flexibility we went directly to the field. First, we wrote to the fifty chief state school officers and two professors of education in each state, asking them to nominate three schools or school districts which, from their own personal knowledge, were implementing procedures to achieve flexibility. We then wrote to the over 300 schools and districts nominated and invited them to describe their programs by completing a Select-O-Sheet questionnaire. Some 225 schools and districts responded. Many supplemented their responses with explanations, or sent pamphlets and brochures. In our cover letter we indicated that we would be inviting brief case study descriptions from a small number of schools and asked each respondent to indicate his willingness to prepare such a statement if asked to do so. Almost all respondents indicated a willingness to write.

After careful study of the questionnaire responses we selected twenty schools and districts representing a wide spectrum of programs throughout the United States. We eliminated some schools because of national publicity already given them in order to point out the large number of schools across America which are adopting procedures to achieve flexibility. We have included in Appendix B a list of all responders classified according to the major thrust of their programs.

This book is not a report of a scientific study. We began by recalling that much of today's literature suggests that to become more effective and more relevant schools must become more flexible. The questions we attempted to address were: How is this flexibility achieved? At what price? With what results? In examining the materials assembled we soon discovered that we would have to arrive at some definitions of procedures. This we have attempted to do.

Are the procedures described in this book actually taking place?

Everyone who has attempted to implement new procedures in schools knows full well that, despite the planning and energy given to implementation, new practices often fall short of expectations. In communicating with the contributors to the volume we pleaded for candidness in their descriptions, urging that the book reflect "the state of the art as it is, imperfect though it might be."

We wish to acknowledge the assistance of 125 professors and chief state school officers who served as nominators of schools for our survey. Without their enthusiastic participation this book would never have been written. We wish also to acknowledge the help received from Jack A. Lown, Executive Director, Minnesota School Facilities Council, Minneapolis, Minnesota, who invited us to review the vast amount of materials he has collected over the past several years on schools across the country. We express our appreciation to Mrs. Mary Ann Jones and Mrs. Marje Logan, who worked feverishly and competently to get the manuscript typed properly. Finally, we acknowledge the help of our wives, Beth and Virginia, who gave valuable assistance in organizing responses and who put up with us throughout the project.

Willard J. Congreve
George J. Rinehart

Contents

Chapter

Appendices

I

Overview of Programs

Willard J. Congreve
and George J. Rinehart

Introduction

Ever since J. Lloyd Trump engaged in his staff utilization studies just prior to 1960, many schools and school districts throughout America have been searching for ways to become more flexible. Flexibility in schools can have different meanings. Usually it is a means to adapt to the multifarious needs of young people. However, it can also be synonomous with bandwagoning, keeping up with the Joneses, or new programs designed to gain recognition, or to assure the school board and public that the schools are not stagnant.

In this book, we have defined flexibility to mean options available to students, teachers, consultants, administration, or others connected with the school, which provide learning opportunities to children which otherwise would not be possible.

As we examined the number and kinds of procedures, we were awed by the large number and also by the fact that almost no aspect of the school operation has been left untouched. We saw this condition as a special challenge over and beyond that of describing and critiquing the activities going on in the schools in our sample. Therefore, we set about to establish categories of procedures which helped us handle our data and which might be useful to others who subsequently examine the flexibility phenomenon. The fourteen categories, their definitions, and how we went about developing them, are included as Appendix A.

Less than 5 percent of the schools and school districts responding to our questionnaire indicated that they were implementing only one procedure to achieve flexibility. Most schools reported doing several things. The following is a brief review of what schools are actually doing.

As we refer to programs in this chapter, the reader should keep in mind that the descriptions do not include all that is going on in that school or school district. Furthermore, in making reference to them, we do not imply that they are the only ones, the best ones, or necessarily unique.

District-wide Programs

Our letters inviting a response to our questionnaire were directed to either individual schools or school districts depending upon the recommendation received from our nominators. In some instances, district-wide staff selected one or a few schools and asked them to respond to the inquiry. In other instances, district-wide staff felt inclined to respond for the entire district, indicating that certain procedures were in effect in many or all schools in the district, or that it was the intention that these procedures would be implemented within the foreseeable future. We turn first to these examples.

Beaverton (Oregon) School District 48 has embarked upon a district-wide project to differentiate its entire staff. The project is a six-year effort which began in 1968 and will be completed in 1974. In moving forward, the district's differentiated staffing committee unanimously accepted the U. S. Office of Education guidelines for differentiated staffing. (1)

The Aloha High School, one of the first Beaverton Schools to adopt differentiated staffing, is housed in a flexible facility with folding walls, independent study carrels, project laboratories, all available to accommodate students during the 40 percent of unstructured time. The curriculum is designed to provide individualized programs during both the classroom and independent study time.

The Cooper Mountain Elementary School embodies such procedures as peer teaching (children teaching other children), cross grade teaching, cross grade grouping, use of high school students and college students, teacher trainers, parent volunteers, and an emphasis on individualized instruction.

The Douglas School System (K-12), Ellsworth Air Force Base, Rapid City (South Dakota) has created an environment which lets children "learn what they want to learn." The teacher (learning facilitator) provides instruction, but it is arranged so that a child or group of children ask the teacher: "how do we do this?" Most students do what all children do, but they do it when and where they want to.

The kindergarten program at Douglas operates in an open building called the Carrousel. It consists of eight classrooms surrounding a multi-purpose central area which is used for a continuous physical education room where children enhance their motor skills and work off their wriggles. The elementary program is conducted in traditional facilities, but there is also offered to parents a demonstration school organized into learning centers: mathematics, language arts, library, drama, art, music, industrial arts, photography, home economics and others. After the children and parents become familiar with the many learning options available, pupil, parent, and teacher cooperatively set goals for each child which then determine his program.

The Douglas High School offers students three types of programs. The "X" program is essentially the usual traditional fare. The "Y" program involves teacher teams and schedules which permit students to pursue a topic in depth rather than on a fixed hourly schedule. Content and objectives are defined by students and teachers. The "Z" program is for the students in grades ten through twelve who are able to direct their own learning. All projects are designed by the individual students in consultation with one or more advisor/teachers assigned to the program.

The Englewood (New Jersey) Public Schools, in a mostly white, suburban, college-oriented community until 1963, faced the major challenge of desegregation through a comprehensive reorganization. This change made possible a flexible, integrated curriculum with room for individual learning preferences. Procedures adopted include: the open classroom, team planning and teaching, various forms of scheduling, open study hall and open campus, independent learning, and diagnostically guided instruction. In assessing the program, the respondent wrote: "At the elementary and middle school levels, where the changes have been established longest, many of the advantages are being realized. At the high school, where most intransigence was found, the effects are just beginning to show."

Mason City (Iowa) elementary schools, called "Unitized Schools," contain three multi-age units: Unit A (ages 5-8), Unit B (ages 8-10), and Unit C (ages 10-12). Through this organization, and the use of differentiated staff, several different groupings for instruction have been created. These include: large groups, small groups, achievement groups, paired learning, and individualized instruction.

The Mason City High School has been on a modular schedule for five years. It is currently adding programs in individually guided education, open study halls, and a partially open campus. Reports indicate improved student attitude, reduced student dropouts, and a threefold increase in library use. Teachers are enthusiastic; their participation in shaping the school has greatly increased.

Size of school district need not be a factor in the degree to which schools adopt procedures to increase flexibility. The Meeker School District, located in remote northwestern Colorado, covers 2000 square miles. Thirty-five percent of its 700 students are transported, some traveling 100 miles per day. A demonstration school district for the Western States Small School Project for Colorado and /I/D/E/A/, Meeker has adopted many procedures to change it from a fairly typical traditional rural school with better than average resources, to an exciting place in which to learn and teach. A relaxed natural relationship exists between students and teachers which encourages the use of more individual talent and creativity on the part of both.

Some 46 procedures distinguish the Meeker curriculum from the fare offered by traditional schools. For example, the district has added vocational exploration, exposure education, and international education (including overseas trips) to "deruralize" its students. To provide for individual learning needs, Meeker uses a modular schedule, team teaching, multi-grade classes, student and adult aides, open study hall and open campus, flexible crediting, interest courses, and individualized materials. The school has unusual educational technology: an educational radio network, amplified telephones, video recorders, audio laboratories, closed circuit TV, and many individually operated mechanisms, including business machines.

A number of other districts reported programs worthy of inspection by persons considering changes on a district-wide basis. Because space does not permit a discussion of all of them, they are listed in Appendix B. This listing probably includes but a fraction of the districts in the United States which are adopting procedures to achieve flexibility. In summary it should be noted that district-wide commitment to such procedures is extremely important if they are to flourish.

Procedures Used to Achieve Flexibility at the Elementary Level

A few common threads run through the responses received from elementary programs. All are committed to becoming more effective in helping individual children succeed despite varying capacities and prior performance. The schools have also adopted several procedures to achieve this flexibility. While many schools offered a title to identify their programs, the title is most often arbitrary. Therefore, we have organized the elementary schools for this discussion according to their major thrust or emphasis as we could discern it.

Instructional Plans to Meet Individual Learning Needs

By far the largest number of elementary school respondents describe their programs as: Instructional Plans to Meet Individual Learning Needs, Diagnostically Guided Prescribed Learning, Individually Guided Education (IGE), or Individually Prescribed Instruction (IPI). The Kettering Foundation /I/D/E/A/ Program has provided funds and considerable influence in helping many of these schools develop their programs.

Thirty-one schools in fifteen states describe their programs in this way. In all but two schools facilities were either constructed or remodeled to provide open spaces where students can work on various tasks. One school, however, has returned to the self-contained classroom, but with an "up-dated attitude" on the part of classroom teachers.

All but one of the schools indicate that team planning and teaching are an essential part of the program. The one school not using this procedure has "one home base teacher acting as a coordinator of student programs with reliance upon assistance from paraprofessionals, teacher aides, and the media specialist." Twenty-three of the 31 schools use some form of differentiated staffing while 24 schools (not including all of the 23) use adults other than teachers on the instructional teams.

All schools reported the use of some form of diagnosis of student learning needs followed by teacher prescription of instructional programs based upon this diagnosis. In about three-fourths of the schools there is some form of student participation in the selection of the learning programs. Half of the schools permit some students to select learning activities in conjunction with their teachers, but only two schools give any students full responsibility for selecting and pursuing learning experiences.

Schools vary in the ways the students are placed into groups. Twenty-two schools place students of multiple age or grade levels together. About half of the schools allow students freedom of movement among the groups, regardless of how they are organized.

All schools expect multiple outcomes from their programs. In addition to achieving greater individualization of the instructional programs, they hope to achieve: accommodations of differential learning needs and preferences (31 schools); opportunities for students to work together to learn from each other (28 schools); greater availability of materials and instructional media (27 schools); opportunities for teachers to work together—to utilize their special talents, to pursue their special interests (27 schools); opportunities to meet the social and emotional needs of children (24 schools); opportunities to use staff of differential background (23 schools).

Three elementary schools use some form of management by objectives. These are computer-managed programs. Subject areas are described by behavioral objectives. Learning experiences for each individual student are determined by prior performance in relationship to the objectives.

While almost all schools have some form of library or resource center, two schools use the learning center essentially as the medium through which individualization is being accomplished. One school has an interesting twist called the "BIG Time Learning Program." Time is planned for each child to learn with a *B*uddy, as an *I*ndividual, and in a *G*roup.

Behavior Modification, a means of using reward systems and contingency contracting, is being used in one school to individualize its program and create effective discipline in the school.

Differentiated Staffing

Four elementary schools reporting have sought flexibility essentially through differentiated staffing. All four have facilities which can be converted to some form of open space. Teachers diagnose and prescribe, usually with some student involvement in the decisions. Students are grouped heterogeneously, often with more than one age or grade level contained within one group. Some of the reported results are encouraging:

> Children have the opportunity to express themselves to a greater degree; teachers can draw upon each other's strengths; they *do* critique each other and improve as a result; individual schools have freedom to adjust staff to suit needs; students are happier and are being provided with more variety of knowledge and unique experiences, and top quality teachers are able to stay in the classroom with increased pay as master teachers instead of leaving for administration posts.

Continuous Progress—Multi-Age Grouping

Twenty elementary schools reporting identified continuous progress or multi-age grouping as the major thrust of their programs. In all but one school, facilities are open space or can be rearranged to provide open spaces. The one exception has a resource center and an audio laboratory. All use team planning and team teaching while 14 utilize some form of differentiated staffing. Seven of the schools did not indicate the use of paraprofessionals, clerks, or volunteers to assist the teachers.

In all twenty schools teachers diagnose learning needs and prescribe learning activities in accordance with these needs. All but two schools involve students in planning learning activities, but only one school allows any students to assume full responsibility in this regard.

All schools group students of more than one age or grade level together, or they allow freedom of movement of students among groups regardless of how they are organized.

The goals being pursued by the schools in this category are essentially the same as those reported for elementary schools in other categories. As to achievements, some of the comments are revealing:

> "Each child achieves daily at his ability and achievement level. School becomes a natural and pleasant place."

"It removes the concept of failure and grade levels."
"We are becoming more proficient in setting goals, adapting learning theories, and using behavioral objectives. We have increased teacher decision-making."
". . . Encourages self-discipline and individual responsibility, for as a student efficiently and diligently fulfills the required tasks he attains more freedom to expand his interests in other areas."

The Open Plan School

Nine elementary schools describe their programs as reflecting the open plan, open classroom, open space concept, open area, or large room design for education. Again these programs differ from the others described previously more in the name given to the program than in the program itself. All pursue essentially the same goals, use multi-age/grade or otherwise heterogeneous grouping, and expect teachers to diagnose learning needs prior to the assignment of learning activities.

The open plan school demands that teachers work together. Four of the nine schools report that they use some form of differentiated staffing. All nine report the use of other adults in addition to certificated teachers.

Procedures Used to Achieve Flexibility in Junior High and Middle Schools

Several common elements exist among all program descriptions received from junior high and middle schools. All refer to staff working together and sharing ideas. They also indicate student involvement of one sort or another. Students are identified as the primary focus of their concern. Those schools which have achieved the greatest range of flexibility also report flexibility in space, such as a pod-type building, an open classroom building, a building with learning or resource centers, or a building especially conducive to the flow and movement of students.

Specific programs and procedures have been reported by some schools such as the Oberon Junior High in Arvada, Colorado. Oberon has developed a "Climate for Inquiry" through a humanizing of the staff, team planning, and various instructional plans to meet individual learning needs. The Brookings (South Dakota) Junior High has created a continuous progress program using team planning, modified differentiated instruction, and flexible grouping. The Burris Laboratory School at Ball State University, Muncie, Indiana, and the South Orange Junior High School of South Orange and Maplewood, New Jersey, have initiated learning centers to provide flexibility in space, materials, and equipment. Such centers are essential to the creation and implementation of programs which include independent learning.

Some junior high and middle schools have described their efforts as primarily team activities of staff and students. The Zion Heights Junior High School in North York, Canada, reports that their open area design facilitated the development of team teaching and flexible grouping.

Classes in the Decatur (Alabama) middle school program are organized into sub-schools or houses-within-a-school. Each grade level is taught by teams of teachers who work together with a common group of students.

The Bell Junior High School in Golden, Colorado, provides multiple learning environments through a democratic organization. It involves students, parents, and teachers in shared decision-making.

Teachers working and planning cooperatively in the Shelbourne (Vermont) Middle School has resulted in several procedures which allow teachers' talents to be maximized. In terms of results, the respondent wrote:

> Some are obvious in that the school no longer has self-contained classrooms; teachers are functioning as members of teams with differentiated roles; the grading system has been replaced by non-quantitative progress reports and parent conferences; reports are made as needed, not at the end of artificial "marking periods." Classes are mostly heterogeneous and fluid of composition. Students are under less pressure.

Through the use of teacher teams, the Oakland Junior High School of Stillwater, Minnesota, has created mini-courses, increased electives, and developed interdisciplinary and individualized programs.

Several junior high and middle schools have looked to scheduling plans to achieve greater flexibility. They have adopted modified versions of the modular schedule which provide more of the things which middle school students seem to require such as: student/teacher contact time, small group instruction, interdisciplinary teaching, diagnosis of student needs, individualized instruction and guided independent study.

They also find that modular scheduling has resulted in more efficient use of teacher time, more opportunities for teachers to work with individual students, an improved library and media center, and resources to create a program for students with problems of social maladjustment.

The Pleasantville (New York) Middle School has moved beyond the flexible modular schedule. Through the use of the matrix technique, it has created individual programs with internal flexibility.

Teachers and students are quite involved in the process. The result comes probably as close as possible to providing true individualized instruction.

Janesville (Wisconsin) Junior High Schools show a somewhat unique thrust to achieve flexibility. One building is an open-pod school which is providing for its students' needs through block-scheduling to departmental teams with instructional plans to meet individual learning requirements. Another school uses an across-subject lines team teaching approach in an open space building. A third has adopted a new 4:1:4 mini-course approach. The traditional two semester program now includes two four-month semesters with one month in between. During this month, students select from a number of mini-courses those which suit their interests. The mini-course program was first launched in January, 1972.

Four other junior high schools responding described their programs as "comprehensive total school commitments" to provide for the learning needs of individual children.

The Meadowbrook Junior High in Newton, Massachusetts, labels its program a "Focus on the Individual." Team planning and teaching and an individualized student-teacher relationship (each of its 882 students has an individual teacher who serves as an advisor), enable the school to meet each student's learning needs.

Oak Grove Junior High in Bloomington, Minnesota, one of the more rare instances of a school which began its program using many varied approaches, summarizes its multi-dimensional program this way:

> It centers on the child, more individually. It brings more human resources and more varied materials to the learning situation. It involves the staff more completely in the total school process, making them more responsive and responsible to students. It involves the school in teacher preparation. It provides flexibility in facilities, resources, and instructional modes.

Procedures to Achieve Flexibility in the High School

Despite the similarities among the high schools in our sample we have grouped the schools to facilitate discussion. We have chosen four groups: organization, continuous progress, scheduling, and various plans to individualize instruction.

Achieving Flexibility through Organization

Three high schools reported the use of unique organizational techniques to achieve flexibility. The secondary programs in the

Lowndes County Schools, Voldosta, Georgia, have found that a twelve-week quarter system enables them to: accommodate students who drop in and out of school, revise the curriculum with ease, and utilize teaching talents more efficiently.

The Okemos (Michigan) High School uses nine-week courses for eleventh and twelfth grade students and allows students to select both their teachers and courses.

Columbia High School, South Orange, New Jersey, is using a Three-House Plan Organization to offset the depersonalization and reduction of leadership opportunities which occur when high schools become larger. Sophomores spend 75 percent of their time taking courses "in the house," juniors 50 percent, and seniors 25 percent.

Achieving Flexibility through Continuous Progress

Two high schools described their programs as "continuous progress." The Conway (Arkansas) High School operates on the unit basis, with students progressing from one unit to the next only after passing the unit. This plan, combined with the summer vacation has created some problems. Currently if a student wants to carry over work from one year to the next, he must go to summer school or he will receive credit only for the semesters of work completed.

The Woodlake Union High Schook, Woodlake, California, states that its students are able to finish a course and start another regardless of semester or yearly controls. "The advanced students proceed rapidly and the slower students have the necessary time to attain completion and success."

Achieving Flexibility through Scheduling

Fifteen high schools located in thirteen states identified scheduling in one form or another (usually modular) as the predominant procedure being used to achieve flexibility. This procedure, now well-known to school schedule makers, has been handled differently by individual schools. Mitchell Senior High School in Colorado Springs, Colorado, reports that they are using it as a vehicle to introduce mini-courses and to create a "school within a school" to help those students who are having difficulty adjusting to the unstructured time aspects of their program. This will not be a "return to structure," but rather will use an interdisciplinary team to meet individual needs.

The Hopkins and Eisenhower Senior High Schools in Hopkins, Minnesota, have added Computerized Achievement Monitoring in social studies, mathematics, biology, and in other departments to a limited degree.

Modular scheduling requires the adoption of several other procedures. Fourteen of the fifteen schools use some form of team planning and teaching. Six report the use of differentiated staffing. Thirteen are housed in buildings which provide some form of open space. One is housed in conventional classrooms, and one permits students to move freely to and from study halls, the library, and student commons, or to leave the campus. Only five schools include volunteers, aides, or paraprofessionals in the instructional program. This evidence indicates a marked reduction in the use of such personnel over the practices in the elementary school.

In fourteen schools teachers diagnose learning needs prior to the assignment of learning activities. In twelve of these schools students participate in determining their assignments; depending upon student ability and self-direction, six schools are willing to give students the major responsibility for this decision.

Examples of results give an indication of what these scheduling procedures are said to accomplish:

1) Students have a positive outlook toward education.
2) The atmosphere of the school has changed so that it seems much less oppressive to students.
3) There is more participation of students in the learning process.
4) There is greater availability of resources, both human and inanimate.
5) Teachers are being released to perform professional tasks; students are helped to become more responsible for their learning.

Achieving Flexibility through Instructional Plans to Meet Individual Learning Needs

Thirty high schools in twenty-two states and the Caroline Islands state their programs are attempting to achieve individualized instruction. A somewhat unusual approach to meet individual needs was the one-time experiment of the Whitman High School in Bethesda, Maryland, in Free Form Education. This program was student-initiated, planned, and administered. It used community persons functioning as teachers, parents as volunteer teachers, and teachers teaching courses outside their major area (such as the French teacher who taught fencing). It involved nearby universities, TV studios, advertising agencies, elementary schools and other community facilities as learning stations.

This one-time activity of a relatively short duration (they never intended to repeat it) had a major impact upon the normal high school program. As a result, new courses were introduced, an extended study project was instituted, parental involvement increased, and the student government was reformed.

A similar but continuing program is in operation at the Burris Laboratory High School, Ball State University, Muncie, Indiana. During three one-week periods throughout each year, the school disbands its normal operations. Students, with parents accepting responsibility, determine the goals of their programs, select the place of study (classroom, community, state or nation), and the resource persons and materials needed to carry out the inquiry.

North Kansas City High School, Kansas City, Missouri, has adopted a Personalized Project Program which enables students to pursue projects of individual interest in depth. In another attempt to break with traditional practices within the self-contained classroom, the high school in Lamar County, Vernon, Alabama, has implemented a "Social Studies for the Seventies" program, centering around problem solving and inquiry.

To develop responsible behavior in students through decision-making, the Dover, New Hampshire, High School has implemented an optional study hall procedure. Students have freedom to choose where they will be during those times when they do not have a scheduled class or an appointment with a teacher.

Five high schools reported varied practices in curriculum to meet individual needs. Nova, Fort Lauderdale, Florida, has created an interrelated math-science curriculum to increase relevancy in both subjects for students. The Cedartown, Georgia, High School has instituted a vocational program which is interlocked with the academic.

The Nashua, Montana, High School uses a multi-media approach in teaching mathematics. The English program at Bellafonte, Pennsylvania, High School uses nongraded groupings, with student selection of six-week mini-courses. About fifty mini-courses are available. Teachers, assigned to their areas of competence and affinity, are better organized and more satisfied.

J. Lloyd Trump and the National Association of Secondary School Principals (NASSP) deserve considerable credit for their influence in encouraging high schools to adopt practices to achieve flexibility. Several schools indicated their involvement as a Model NASSP Project School, or a "Trump Plan" school. Perhaps the best way for the reader to get a flavor of these schools is from the comments of the respondents regarding their achievements.

The Patrick Henry Senior High School in San Diego, California, is increasing student participation in planning learning activities so that each graduate will have a marketable skill. The Samoa High School in the Caroline Islands is stressing culturally relevant materials, tests, and learning situations. The Salina (Kansas) High School uses individual achievement related to individual ability as the primary basis for student evaluation. Red Basin High School in Grand Forks,

North Dakota, has created a "Program of Responsibility" which enables students to schedule their activities on a weekly rather than a semester basis.

Courses at Athens High School in The Plains, Ohio, are organized into five phases. A phase one course is for students who are far behind and need personal attention, while a phase five course is for students who are competent to comprehend college-level work in high school. The student chooses the phase he desires, using test scores, previous grades and teacher recommendations. This responsibility has been placed on the student with considerable success.

Six high schools reported rather unusual programs. The Clear Creek Secondary School in Idaho Springs, Colorado, places each student on a contract after the student and teacher agree on what should be included. The contract can be changed if this becomes necessary. A released-time contract can also be drawn up which allows the student to leave the campus to pursue other learning experiences in the community. While most learners assume responsibility for pursuing their education, there is considerable frustration and apprehension on the part of some because directions are not always clear.

The Murray Road Annex for eleventh and twelfth graders in Newton, Massachusetts, provides an opportunity for students to accept responsibility for both their education and the operation of the school. There is no administration. Aides, interns, student teachers, and parents supplement the core faculty of eight who work with 117 randomly selected students.

The ultimate purposes of Murray Road are summed up in the following statement:

> We want students to enjoy learning; to seek our resources within the school and outside; to grow in self-confidence, initiation, curiosity, excitement, and a sense of responsibility to themselves and others. We want students to begin a process of self-education which can continue throughout their lives.

Shawnee Mission (Kansas) Northwest High School has created a program to involve students in making decisions about all aspects of the school. (2) They have a major voice in dress codes, the use of bells, study hall passes, vending machines, music for the student center, and course offerings. Currently students are developing a proposal to eliminate the "F" grade and substitute a Pass-Withdrawal plan. Plans are being drawn for students to evaluate teachers to help them reach students more effectively. Northwest reports reduced vandalism, increased student attendance, a high level of student morale, and positive identification with the school.

Hortons Wathens High School in St. Louis, Missouri, provides students the option of studying under a traditional plan or the

Innovation Program. Under the latter, the student may proceed at his own rate in all subjects, he may be excused from formal class meetings with the teacher's permission, or he may plan his own course of study for a subject. The number of students choosing innovative classes has grown tremendously. Test scores of the best students have improved, and library usage has gone up 200 percent. While not all students use their independent time wisely, feedback from graduates reveals that they feel better prepared for higher learning than the majority of their college classmates.

The Archbishop Ryan High School (parochial) in Omaha, Nebraska, has implemented a Learning by Appointment program. There are no schedules, no grades. Students have optional attendance on Wednesday and also optional attendance during the last semester of the high school program. The program meets individual needs more immediately and places responsibility for learning squarely upon the student. "It is more humane."

The Herricks Public School District in New Hyde Park, New York, has just implemented a modified "free school" for the eleventh and twelfth graders. Involving resources of the community, the curriculum is organized into four divisions: aesthetics, communications, human relations, and technology. Students have complete freedom to attend classes, seminars, and other meetings inside and outside of school. Both day and evening meetings are held. Some students may leave the school entirely for a period of time for independent work or study.

It would be inappropriate to pass over the John Adams High School located in Portland, Oregon. This school, opened in 1969, was designed by a team of educators prior to its opening. (3) Its goals included:

1) Providing an educational experience relevant to the needs and interests of all adolescents, regardless of their intentions to pursue further formal education.
2) Developing a commitment to fundamental democratic principles and the development of a capacity to work within those principles to effect environmental change.
3) Enabling students to experience and explore a fuller range of human relationships than is typical in schools.

Only one school places the emphasis upon the use of differentiated staffing. This school, which shall remain anonymous, reported a significant problem contronting schools which attempt to adopt procedures different from what has traditionally been the routine. The respondent wrote:

Due to a recent administrative change, our program has changed as well. The information on the Select-O-Sheet probably reflects some of the old and new.

But I must admit that we seem to be turning toward a more traditional and conventional program . . . .

Special Programs for Special Needs

Our survey identified schools which are addressing their entire school programs to unique needs. While each school merits considerable description, we can only whet the appetite of the reader.

Parkway High School, Philadelphia, established the concept of using the community as its school. Parkway has no building; all courses are taught in community facilities. Several versions of the Parkway have developed in other large cities, such as Chicago and Baltimore. Much smaller school districts like Williston, North Dakota, and Newton, Iowa, are finding ways to use the community to enrich instructional offerings, increase relevancy in their programs, and build career education into the curriculum. (4)

The Ponape Agriculture and Trade School located in the Caroline Islands, uses community resources in its career education program. To help students to develop self-confidence, the school offers courses in mechanics, construction, agriculture, and work experience. The work experience is directed by highly proficient tradesmen who do not have academic credentials, while the classwork is taught by credentialed teachers.

Schools and special programs have been established to encourage students to remain in school. A major portion of these programs has a manual and tactile orientation. Seneca, South Carolina, High School has an adjunct program (Project Succeed) for ninth and tenth grade potential dropouts. They are taught by specially trained teachers, in smaller classes set up in laboratory settings where the work is adjusted to former achievement levels. Students *have* to succeed if they try. Student attitude has improved and dropouts have been reduced.

Denver, Colorado, has its Metropolitan Youth Education Center which provides instruction and personalized counseling in small classes (8-12 students) for persons in grades 10-12, ages 16 to 25. The program, in effect since 1964, is having a fair measure of success.

Baltimore, Maryland, has a special program to insure that teenage mothers will continue their education. The program provides a school environment where the girls are socially accepted and where they can continue their studies without interruption.

The Vern W. Furgeson, K-6 School in Hawaiian Gardens, California, began an unusual year-round program in September, 1971. Attendance is on a quasi-volunteer basis, in that students are required to attend 178 days a year, but could go for 220 days. Teacher and staff vacations are staggered throughout the year. The program, essentially continuous progress, with students grouped heterogeneously by age for instruction, is designed to reach the migrant population prevalent in the area.

Year-round schools are by no means new. Baltimore, Chicago, and other large cities have begun pilot projects. The leader in this field is probably Atlanta, Georgia.

An unusual private school effort is the Learning Village in Kalamazoo, Michigan. The Village provides a highly structured non-failure environment for children, ages 2 months to 12 years. The student body is diverse socially and socio-economically. There are no grade levels. The program is based entirely on behavioral objectives vertically constructed in the learning areas. Students master prerequisites at the 100 percent level before moving on. No remediation is needed.

A quite different private school is the Prospect School in North Bennington, Vermont. Operated in collaboration with Bennington College, the school borrows heavily from the integrated day concept of the British infant, primary and junior school. Great emphasis is placed upon the use of manipulative materials. Students pursue learning which originates entirely from their expressed interests, with teachers acting as guides.

Community involvement has been evident in many of the programs mentioned thus far. However, this involvement is becoming much more intense in various places across the country. A forerunner of community involvement was Flint, Michigan. With the assistance of the Charles Stewart Mott Foundation, the Flint Board of Education created the attitude in Flint where the citizens feel that school buildings are theirs to enjoy and use. Opening the buildings at night and over the weekend, has enabled over 90,000 people to engage in self-improvement programs.

Baltimore (Maryland) used a community charette approach to design its new Dunbar High School, scheduled to be opened in 1975. Des Moines (Iowa) used a similar approach to design some of its new inner city schools which are now under construction.

East Baton Rouge (Louisiana) has a day-evening program for students 16 years and older. They are permitted to arrive and leave the campus whenever they desire, taking whatever courses they desire. West Side High School in Gary, Indiana, involves students, staff, and parents in openly structured confrontation. Actual individual and community problems, and the methods developed to attack them, are the main elements in the CORE curriculum.

Special Education

Five respondents described special education programs dealing with the educable mentally retarded (EMR), specific learning disabilities and the emotionally disturbed child. As in other programs, the main emphasis is to provide for the individual needs of the child. Current trends in EMR programs are to keep the child integrated into the regular classroom with a specially trained Child Resource Teacher assigned to the building to help the classroom teacher deal with learning problems. For children with learning disabilities and emotional problems, help or treatment is provided through learning centers, resource teachers, or specially structured environments. Most efforts attempt to return the child to the school mainstream in the shortest possible time.

Most respondents indicated that the academic achievement of the special education student was at least as good in the new program as in the previously used segregated programs. Further, they felt the new approaches developed more humane, civilized, and responsible children.

Early Childhood Education

A few respondents described early childhood education programs usually operating in collaboration with day-care enterprises. Strong parent involvement in planning, operating, and evaluation was a characteristic of the program. "Alternative" schools were being developed in some urban areas. One program described parents being trained to be "teachers" of the child at home, as an alternative to the traditional kindergarten program.

Achieving Flexibility— Some General Problems

How Are These Programs Being Evaluated?

School boards and educators attempting to implement procedures to increase flexibility are faced with the question: "How is this better than what has been done in the past?" or, from more tolerant patrons, "How are you going to evaluate this program?"

Knowing that our respondents had undoubtedly faced these questions, we asked them to describe the procedures being used to determine the effectiveness of their programs. The responses confirm the suspicion that considerable effort is needed to develop means to gather sufficient and convincing evidence to determine if the procedures used and the flexibility gained are indeed contributing positively to the educational development of the children. The problem is not assessing the degree of flexibility achieved. Rather it is determining the effect of the flexibility achieved on the educational outcomes.

Two major issues compound this latter problem. The first is philosophical. If one views education as a strict, rigid, training process, predetermined and systematically carried out by school staff, he must reject as self-defeating any procedures which loosen up this process. On the other hand, if one views education as a process capable of attaining several goals, then agreement as to goals being sought must be reached before evaluation can begin.

The second issue is a technical one. Once the goals have been agreed upon, what system of measurement and evaluation should be employed? Fairly precise normative tools are available in the limited areas of basic skills, knowledge attainment, and, to some extent, in the ability of students to use skills and apply knowledge. However, as one seeks to measure and evaluate the less tangible behaviors in the affective domain, the tools become quite scarce.

Less convincing procedures have been developed to assess critical thinking, attitude towards self and school, enthusiasm, pride, humaneness, learning how to learn, morale, etc. Most people would agree that these behaviors exist, but measuring them is difficult.

Nevertheless, if a thing exists it should be measurable, at least approximately. Measurement can be direct or through inference. We suggest that more skill and confidence is needed in the use of observation, anecdotal records, rating scales, questionnaires, and interviews. Even such intangibles as empirical "feels" have some meaning in evaluation, especially in those situations which seem to defy specific identification and measurement. The following examples of procedures described by our respondents reveal the status of evaluation techniques available to assess these programs.

Elementary schools reporting have used the usual standardized tests, but immediately recognize the inadequacy of these to measure other important outcomes. In order to get at these behaviors, schools are recording examples of children's behavior and attempting to relate them to attitude. In addition, questionnaires to parents, staff, and children, observation reports from other teachers, and outside assessments by university personnel are being attempted. Some schools frankly report that "no formal evaluation instrument has been used," or "I have only the feeling of the school, plus comparing this school with other schools." And, "After the program has been operating for a few years, we'll ask our junior high school to participate in a comparative study of student strengths before and after the program was instituted."

The statement on evaluation of the Rincon School in Livermore, California, pretty well sums up what other elementary schools are doing:

Most evaluation instruments (other than standardized achievement tests) are in the form of questionnaires to teachers, parents, and visitors. They are based upon observation, or conclusions drawn from our own experience or what we know about the experience of others in similar situations.

Junior high schools report using procedures similar to those used in elementary schools. Somewhat more emphasis is placed upon achievement tests, but other measures such as attendance and tardiness records, number of students who show up in counselors' offices with problems, and community feedback are providing what seem to be useful data. Few schools are in the position of the Oak Grove Junior High School, Bloomington, Minnesota, which had an outside formal assessment of its program for each of the first two years and is planning an extensive evaluation which will cost about $10,300.

Evaluation procedures used by senior high schools are little different from those described above. Dropout data, success of students in college, and satisfactory adjustment of graduates in the world of work are also used. Community reaction and response seem to provide important data.

Perhaps the plan being used by the Lowndes County School District in Voldosta, Georgia, is about the best we can expect at the moment. It involves: using specific objectives as test items, informal student interviews, community reaction as revealed in the news media, and on-site visitations by other school systems and State Department officials.

Problems Encountered in Implementation

Although change is necessary to achieve flexibility, most of us seem to have a built-in resistance to it. Our questionnaire requested information regarding the difficulties schools encountered in implementing new procedures. We asked about problems with staff, students, parents, the community, and facilities. Respondents were asked to check those items which had been problems, and were invited to add other items, or expand upon the ones checked.

Staff acceptance and commitment proved to be problems in several instances. "The usual resistance to change" item was checked by more than 45 percent of those responding. About 30 percent also identified "converting the lone wolf to a member of a professional team" as a problem. Between 25 and 30 percent of the respondents noted as problems: staff unfamiliarity, lack of commitment to particular purposes, and unbelief in the potential of students. Failure to realize the need for a multi-dimensional learning environment rather than a different kind of unidimensional setting, appeared to be a problem for several schools.

Twenty percent of the respondents cited staff fears about loss of security or position, indicating the necessity for a reasonable transition period when moving to a new program. However, conditions should be established so that teachers cannot refuse to change. Mistrust of administration and an unwillingness to have results of work on display was noted in 10 percent of the replies. However, less than 5 percent of the schools identified organized opposition of unions or teacher groups as a problem.

Some reported other problems, such as the large amount of extra time and work required of staff in planning and implementing flexible programs. A few felt some staff wanted to move too fast. Many commented that because staff were specially selected and trained for the new tasks, little difficulty was experienced by them.

With regard to students, almost one-half of the respondents indicated that a reasonable transition period would have helped students adapt more effectively to the changes made. Some schools have attempted to move too rapidly with too little orientation for the young people. There seems to be a need for a smooth, orderly, transition period. Students who are conditioned to an unidimensional learning environment or have differential learning preferences sometimes find it next to impossible to be productive in open learning situations.

About 15 percent of the respondents suggested that some students lack skills necessary to enter new programs and others have personal needs which demand competition with fellow students. Several responses indicated that while students are adaptable to change, there are some who find it difficult to accept the responsibility for their own learning. Involving students in developing plans for implementing procedures seemed to be a great help.

Parents and communities often have predetermined ideas about education which cause problems in implementing procedures different from those to which they are accustomed. Fifty percent of the schools responding had parents who felt children were too young to make decisions regarding their own learning and need to be told what to do. Approximately 25 percent reported opposition from parents who felt that learning for all students requires a definite pace and a specific sequence. In addition they felt competition to be essential as this is the only way children will learn how to come out ahead in the competitive market place. More than 15 percent reported other community attitudes creating difficulties: each child must have his own teacher; to be treated fairly all children should get the same treatment; flexible programs are not teaching all the children.

Individual comments show that some parents believe that learning cannot and should not be enjoyable; they want school as they remember it. "I was taught this way, teach my kids this way." Other parents, apparently conditioned to textbooks and grades, feel that students today learn less than in the good old days. One respondent concluded: "Improving communication with the community and clearing up rumors should be the number one goal of many school districts." Other responses indicate that the more involved and informed the community the better the chance for success of any new program.

Problems created by facilities are not as serious as they have often been made out to be. Approximately 40 percent of the schools report that staff use the lack of a specific facility as an excuse for not implementing a certain procedure. While some procedures obviously work better in specially designed facilities, many are being carried out in a traditional building.

However, almost 40 percent pointed out that school boards, administrators, and teachers, often fail to realize the vast amount of materials needed to implement flexible programs. Furthermore, facilities are often designed without involving staff. Teachers who lack expertise in using flexible facilities often have trouble. A building specifically designed and staffed for the procedures used eliminates many of the problems accompanying implementation.

At least 75 percent of the responding schools are using staff planning groups, community involvement activities and consultants to overcome the opposition. Allowing staff to attend seminars and workshops held by consulting firms and universities has also been helpful. Some districts deliberately changed facilities to bring about a change in teacher behavior. Almost 10 percent admit to effecting change by administrative edict, or, as one respondent put it, "administrative guidance." A number of schools encourage their staff to visit schools using flexible procedures. One administrator stated that the most important factor in overcoming any problem is the energy and devotion of good teachers who pride themselves in their work and put students first.

The extent to which procedures to improve flexibility are being implemented is at best a calculated guess. About half of the schools responding indicate new programs operating in one or a few schools in their district. System-wide programs were reported by about 25 percent of the school districts, and 15 percent indicate that only certain teachers are involved. Lacking interpretation and clarification, this information is of limited value. The size of the district makes considerable difference. Large districts involving a few schools or certain teachers could be reaching more students than are smaller systems with district-wide efforts. Moreover, a district-wide commitment is no guarantee that full implementation is occurring in every classroom. It does appear, though, that as procedures to improve flexibility are being implemented across the country and as programs demonstrate success, they are soon adapted to additional schools.

How Are These Programs Financed?

Most respondents indicate that their programs are funded through the local operational budget at no greater cost than the usual programs. Securing the amount and variety of instructional materials needed while operating within the normal budget is often a problem, however. Some felt they were acquiring the reputation of "scroungers." One respondent answered the question about funding with, "Ha!" Some obviously have need for more funds. A substantial number of schools report their projects were originally supported under Title III of ESEA (Elementary and Secondary Education Act) and EPDA (Education Professions Development Act) funds have been used quite extensively for training purposes. There is little doubt that federal funding has been effective in helping plan and implement procedures to improve flexibility in schools. A few schools received support from private foundations.

What Seems to Be the Future of These Programs?

To answer this question we asked the schools to assess the permanence of goals being pursued and whether these goals represent a fundamental change in thinking or merely reflect the times. These questions brought a wide variety of responses. Most schools indicate that the goals of their project are permanent. Several felt their programs reflected a fundamental change in thinking, but an equal number said that the goals did not change much, merely methods and techniques, "enabling us to more nearly achieve our goals." Some suggested that self-direction in student learning is a newer aspect of the goals being pursued.

Inasmuch as future depends somewhat upon outcome, measurement of effect is a serious concern. Almost everyone responding agrees that definitive outcomes are difficult to measure accurately. While students in the new programs are gaining academically or doing as well as formerly when measured by standardized tests, these outcomes are rarely considered the most important achievements. Learning how to learn, diagnosis and prescriptive teaching, a humanized learning environment, responsibility, self-direction, and happier kids are the objectives sought. But, as pointed out earlier, measurement of these behaviors is still a problem.

What Role Has Teacher Education Played?

Teacher education institutions get differential report cards on their success in producing teachers to staff flexible programs. Schools working closely with a teacher education institution are quite complimentary. While some of these colleges are not seen as leading the way in preparing teachers for new programs, they are working with schools needing such teachers and are changing their programs slowly. Many schools provide student teaching stations and thus expose prospective teachers to future needs.

Some respondents felt that teacher educators are "dragging their feet." They may be "amenable but too fossilized to change," and are still preparing traditional teachers. However, this may not be entirely the fault of the institutions, because most schools still want traditional teachers. Some expressed the opinion that before any great change can occur in teacher education, professors must understand and practice individualized instruction in their own classrooms. Intern programs and inservice training are activities which forward-looking teacher education institutions could carry on.

Three replies were received from unique teacher education projects. Graduate students at the Claremont, California, School of Education, plan and operate mini-schools for a six-week period. This provides them an opportunity to experience flexible procedures in actual class situations. The Palm Beach (Florida) County Schools have produced self-study, programmed materials and video tape lessons designed to "effect a desirable change in teaching habits or methods and allow transference from one subject area to another." This individualized in-service program, IN-STEP, is a special ESEA Title III project. Modules of this course present materials covering psychological foundations, objectives, goals, behavioral hierarchies, needs assessment, individualized instruction, and instructional systems.

What About Teacher Organizations?

Most procedures to achieve flexibility require different performance behaviors from teachers. Are teacher organizations willing to consider options to the "treat us all the same" philosophy of uniform performance expectations and salary schedule? Will they support differentiated assignments for teachers with accompanying differentiation in pay? Most respondents readily admitted "I don't know," but were optimistic. Little opposition to their projects had been encountered. "Involvement, the key to acceptance," is the idea which schools report most often. Good teachers know what is right for children and support programs to help students.

Some replies did point out the conflict between the union push for a shorter work day and the fact that individual flexible programs require more time. One respondent suggested that the "treat us all the same" philosophy was needed to enable teachers to reach a decent place in society, but that it should not go on indefinitely. The profession must eventually accept differentiation of reward for ability as inevitable and just. The current teacher surplus was identified as a factor which would affect the attitude of teacher organizations.

Nevertheless, there appears to be little opposition to differentiated assignment or to some differentiation of pay at the local level. Those teachers involved in such projects are supportive. It appears that teachers will accept and support such plans if they are involved, consulted, and assured of the proper evaluation procedures, and if the programs offer children better opportunities to learn. However, differentiation of assignment which tends to reduce the number of certified staff may meet opposition.

Notes

(1) "Second Year Proposal, Request for Grant under Education Professions Development Act of 1967, submitted by Beaverton School District 48, Washington County, Beaverton, Oregon 1970-71," (mimeographed).
(2) The Shawnee Mission Northwest High School is discussed in: Bill Ray Lewis, "An Innovative High School in a Midwestern Suburb," *Phi Delta Kappan,* Vol. LIII, No. 2, October, 1971, pp. 105-107.
(3) For an account of the history of John Adams High School, see Robert B. Schwartz, *et al.,* "The John Adams High School" and other related articles in *Phi Delta Kappan,* Vol. LII, No. 9, May, 1971, pp. 514-530.
(4) For a description of the program in Newton, see Chapter IV in this volume.

II

Project *CREATES* and the Exploratory Learning Center (ELC) in Tucson

Ronald L. DeWitt

In September 1969, Tucson (Arizona) Public Schools, District 1, opened a fifty-year-old elementary school building as an Exploratory Learning Center for the purpose of exploring innovative programs. These programs are intended to be of limited duration, being replaced after sufficient time for evaluation and dissemination. Certain features have been built into the ELC in an effort to remove some of the obstacles which hamper innovative programs:

1) *Student enrollment is voluntary.* Neighborhood children may attend either the ELC or other nearby schools. Children from other parts of the district may apply for enrollment.
2) *Teachers work at the Center voluntarily.* Teachers assigned to the ELC are selected from among those who prefer to be assigned there.
3) *Research and dissemination* are built-in functions of any project that is approved for implementation in the Center.
4) *Administrative organization* includes an Advisory Council, Executive Board, Center Director, Administrative Intern and Research Assistant.

The school is on the fringe of the Tucson downtown area and lies one-half mile from the University of Arizona which is expanding into the area served by the school. Currently 36 percent of the 410 students reside in the neighborhood area and 64 percent in other parts of the district. This mix gives the Center a distribution of ethnic groups which virtually matches that of the total district: American Indian 1 percent, Oriental 2 percent, Negro 5 percent, Mexican-American 30 percent, Anglo and others 62 percent.

Project CREATES (Cultural Resources Exploration: Awareness Through Educating the Senses)

The current program, Project CREATES, is the first innovative program being studied at the Center. The theories behind Project CREATES were developed by Dr. Nathan I. Krevitsky, Director of Art for the Tucson Public Schools. In 1966, he received an ESEA Title III planning grant to collect background information in support of his theories and to develop plans for a large museum-like center (CREATES Center). Unfortunately the CREATES Center concept proved too costly to bring into realization; therefore the idea was tabled.

In the fall of 1969, the Exploratory Learning Center was opened and CREATES emerged as the project having the greatest potential. The plan was redesigned so that it could be implemented in an elementary school. Teachers, parents, and administrators were invited to a series of weekly meetings to discuss Dr. Krevitsky's ideas, and, in the Spring of 1970, a Title III proposal was submitted. It was approved for funding to begin July 1, 1970.

Prior to the beginning of the project, a four-week workshop for teachers was conducted. Two main purposes for the workshop were to acquaint teachers in greater depth with the CREATES concepts, and to involve the teachers directly in developing the organizational pattern for implementing the project. From this beginning has come a program which, through evaluation and refinement, has gathered strength and community support.

Project CREATES has four major goals:

1) To demonstrate that working with children in more open ways is an effective way of achieving skills and attitudes valued in our society.
2) To allow children to become responsibly self-directing.
3) To allow children to become more aware of themselves and their total environment.
4) To develop and improve basic skills.

The Organization of Project CREATES

Classrooms are set up as centers where certain kinds of activities take place. Considerable overlapping exists and a high degree of interrelationship has developed. Fundamentally, three kinds of centers have evolved as a result of the first year's experience: Base Centers, CREATES Centers, and Work Centers.

Base Centers. The Base Center provides each child a homeroom, a basic skills area, and a teacher who is responsible for supervising his educational program. In the ELC there are four Base Centers:

kindergarten, grades 1-2-3, grades 2-3, and grades 4-5-6. Table 1 shows the number of participants in each center.

TABLE 1

Number of Participants in Base Centers

Base	Children in Grades							Total	Adults	
	K	1	2	3	4	5	6		Teachers	Tchr. Aides
Kindergarten	47	-	-	-	-	-	-	47	1	0
1-2-3	-	64	20	12	-	-	-	96	2	2
2-3	-	-	49	54	-	-	-	103	2	2
4-5-6	-	-	-	-	67	50	47	164	3	2
Totals	47	64	69	66	67	50	47	410	8	6

The homeroom functions are the responsibility of eight Base Center teachers. Five other teachers have no homeroom responsibility. Activities which are primarily those of the homeroom include attendance accounting, reporting to parents, and helping children work through problems. Children are helped both on an individual basis and through frequent class meetings which have been developed along the lines recommended by Dr. William Glasser. (1)

The term "basic skills" is defined in this program as language arts and mathematics. Individual differences are taken into consideration in the structuring of the basic skills program. Generally speaking, however, each child is required to spend one-third to one-half of his day in the Base Center working on basic skills. For example, a third-grader working out of Base 1-2-3 would be required to spend half of the morning and half of the afternoon in the Base Center, and the remainder of the time he is free to choose from among other activities. No more than half of the children assigned to a base are there at any one time.

CREATES Centers. In writing about his original idea for a museum-like center, Dr. Krevitsky states:

> One aim of the Center is to demonstrate that children learn effectively through experience, experiment, search, research, and discovery . . .
> The principle upon which Project CREATES is based is that of developing progressively from the concrete to the abstract, from intuitive understanding to analysis, from sensory awareness to verbalization, from feeling to thinking, from speaking to writing to reading. (2)

The CREATES Center provides a stimulating atmosphere in which objects, graphics and language combine to introduce concepts which are inviting to children. The Centers are prepared around topics such as earth, time-space-motion, life, color, sound, or energy. These themes are broad in scope so that they are appropriate to all areas of the curriculum. Materials related to the concept of the center are exhibited.

A variety of activities is provided: a staff member from a local zoo brings in animals to share with the children; two girls team up and teach other children how to make macrame; a boy writes a book about the pet snake he is caring for in the center; projectors illuminate a shadow screen while children experiment with shapes as seen in shadows; someone hurries off to the library to find a book about Africa.

The team of adults responsible for the activities in the CREATES Center is made up of two teachers, one teacher-aide, and one art technician. Two classrooms have been converted into CREATES Centers at the ELC. Currently, one has been developed around the concept "Earth" and the other around "Time-Space-Motion." These concepts are starting places which are not intended to limit a child to looking at a topic only in terms of its obvious meaning. Even though a child started with "Earth," he may end up studying outer space.

Children visit the CREATES Center by choice. Nothing in this center is forced on the children, but once they have made a commitment to start a project of exploration or to participate in a group activity, every effort is made to hold them to that commitment. Although flexibility is valued in the school, it is felt that most of the time children will benefit from being held to their decisions.

Work Centers. As with CREATES Centers, children visit the Work Centers of their own accord. One large double room area, the workroom, provides materials and equipment for activities in art, science, cooking, sewing, woodworking, photography, and bookmaking. These activities are supervised by two teachers and two teacher aides. An area in the auditorium provides a place for drama activities in the morning and music in the afternoon. These are conducted by a teacher and one half-day aide. A two-classroom size library provides the program with a third Work Center and is supervised by a librarian and one half-day aide. Physical education is taught outdoors by various teachers in turn.

In the project it is understood that a child may acquire motivation in any available center or that learning to read may result more directly from time spent in homemaking than from sitting in a formal reading group. These are the kinds of results the school values most.

"Facilitator" or "resource person" are terms which describe the role of the teacher working in a CREATES or Work Center. As to content, the teacher is seen as a person who is there to help the child do what he needs and wishes to do. It is often necessary for the teacher to suggest, present, or instruct, but for the child who is ready, the guiding principle is that he be helped in pursuing his own interest.

Procedures to Achieve Flexibility. Several procedures are used in this project to achieve flexibility: fixed-flexible scheduling, the open classroom, individualized learning, unique curricula offerings, mini-courses, team planning and teaching, use of resource people, involvement through shared planning and decision-making, and integration of the physically handicapped. Initially it was not the plan to use any of these methods; they resulted because Dr. Krevitsky's thoughts forced a consideration of children as individual learners and an examination of the circumstances which bring about learning.

Fixed-Flexible Scheduling. Each child has a fixed time when he must be in the Base Center. For younger children this time is equivalent to one-half the day. For the older it is usually one-third of the school day. Children must also sign up for Spanish class, chorus, movies, mini-courses, and guest speakers, which are scheduled at specific times. During the remainder of the day, students are free to choose from among the CREATES or Work Centers. These are open for free, come-and-go visitation on the part of students.

Some children have great difficulty handling the flexible time. Base teachers work more closely with these children. In Base 1-2-3, for example, approximately forty children were kept together initially and visited centers as a group. The teacher in the receiving center had group activities prepared for them and helped them to learn ways of working in the center. Some children returned to the flexible schedule as they demonstrated readiness to use free time.

The Open Classroom. The school building in use was built for a self-contained classroom program. Although some single classroom areas remain, the building was remodeled, providing four double classroom areas, some completely open, others with doorways. These areas are quite satisfactory and can accommodate almost any kind of program desired.

Teams of teachers and aides monitor the activities in the areas. Within the Base Center there is considerable opportunity for movement among various kinds of learning activities. Some are structured for small groups and others for individuals.

Individualized Learning. Individuality is a prime consideration in determining the content and methods to be used. Choice in scheduling activities allows the child to seek *his* interests, pursue satisfaction of *his* own needs.

Unique Curriculum Offerings. Project CREATES goes right to the heart of the curriculum; what it contains and how it is presented are crucial. Among his writings Dr. Krevitsky states:

> The project design approaches education in an unorthodox manner, de-emphasizing the textbook. The experience of learning from things and from the observation of phenomena in action may prove that children learn when the desire to learn is stimulated through sensory exposure and awareness. (3)

It has been possible to break from the textbook almost completely for science, social studies, and health. Textbooks are partially used in the language arts, and mathematics. Use of textbooks in CREATES and Work Centers is virtually nil, but use of books *per se* abounds.

Mini-Courses. Short term courses allow children to explore various areas of interest. Courses such as drum, guitar, melody bells, the recorder, macrame, and bonsai plants have been offered. These are taught by teachers, parents, visitors, or children.

Team Planning and Teaching. Team teaching and open classrooms go hand-in-hand, and a move toward those alternatives was considered desirable. Although the building did not require teaming, it was felt that getting teachers to trust one another enough to share their ideas and abilities could result in an improved educational process. There have been conflicts, but these are the natural result of people coming into contact with one another. What is significant is that the conflicts are being resolved.

Use of Resource People. In a week's time, approximately fifty different individuals perform some kind of volunteer service in the ELC. Volunteers include junior and senior high school students, university students, university professors, parents, and interested citizens. Most work with the children—teaching a mini-course, helping in the library, or assisting in the classroom. Some consult with teachers in such areas as animal care, reading and math. Parents are asked at the beginning of the year to volunteer and are surveyed for special talents, interests, or hobbies they might share with the children and teachers.

Involvement Through Shared Planning and Decision-Making. A continuing policy at the ELC is: "If a person is to be involved in carrying out a decision, he will be involved in making the decision." The Advisory Council recommends general policies. Teachers work as a total staff in determining specific school policies, particularly those of an educational nature. Individual teams make decisions about the operation of their centers, taking care not to disrupt the interrelationship that exists among centers. Parents have two representatives on the Advisory Council, are welcomed at staff meetings, and are encouraged to visit the school as often as they like. The parent sponsored organization provides the school and parents with helpful services, communicates parents' ideas and concerns to the school, and helps the school to communicate with the parents. Children voice their ideas and concerns in class meetings, although the children are probably not listened to as closely as they should be.

Integration of Physically Handicapped. Part of the program which seems to be working out quite well is the integration of thirteen physically handicapped children. These children would ordinarily be in a special education classroom. However, in the Exploratory Learning Center they are full participants. They are assisted by two resource teachers trained in working with the physically handicapped.

How Well Is It Working?

The project is only in its second year, so the following statements are an indication of present status. Formal evaluation is made through the use of structured observations and standardized tests.

Formal and informal observations suggest the following conclusions with respect to student outcomes:

1) Statistically, children show no significant change in their degree of self-directedness. However, several parents reported that they observe their children being more resourceful, more thoughtful in planning, and more independent.
2) On pre- and post-testing in reading and mathematics, the total school group made normal gains, neither excelling beyond nor falling short of what was expected from past performance.
3) Reports from parents and informal observations of the staff indicate that many children have a significantly more positive attitude toward school.
4) Based on the staff's own informal observations, it appears that the needs of boys are more adequately met in a program like this. There are opportunities for them to construct, manipulate, draw, take apart and reassemble. Boys predominate in the use of CREATES Centers and the activities offered there.
5) The structure provides for movement, activity, and conversation among children. Several things result: the noise level is higher, events which have been traditionally viewed as "discipline problems" occur and must be coped with, and there is more untidiness, more mess, more trash and litter.
6) Some children continue to wander aimlessly during flexible time. They avoid confrontation with adults, apparently wishing to avoid doing anything productive.

With respect to what is called "process outcomes" the following has been noted:

1) Teacher attitudes have been influenced; they express concern about the possibility of having to work in a more traditional program again.
2) Hundreds of visitors' comments also support the conclusions that the Center has had some positive influence in shaping teacher attitudes.
3) It is being demonstrated that an old building can be used for developing new programs.
4) An effective system for adequately teaching physical education within the current organizational structure is yet to be found.
5) The Center is not yet doing all of the things it ultimately hopes to be doing in terms of Dr. Krevitsky's ideas.

6) Time for planning and preparation continues to be inadequate, and is one of the more serious limitations.

Financing of the Project

Tucson Public Schools, District #1, provides the school with the amount usually allotted to an elementary school. In addition, funding for an administrative intern, a half-time research assistant, and research and dissemination from the district is received. ESEA Title III has provided: $78,845 the first year; $65,097 the second year; approximately $32,000 the third year. Plans are to reduce the cost of the project so that after the third year, when the federal funding ceases, all costs can be assumed by the district.

The Future

The potential for continuation and expansion of this program is very high. It exists in a district which encourages and nourishes thoughtful, innovative ideas. Members of the university faculty have been especially helpful. Those working in the project are dedicated and committed to the program objectives. The assistance and backing of the parents has been highly gratifying.

Nevertheless, two major questions remain: (1) Can the cost of the program be reduced to the level of normal district financing without damaging the effectiveness of the program? (2) Will the project ideas take hold in other schools in the district to create a lasting influence?

The major item of concern in the Title III budget is the allocation for teacher aides. To solve this problem, during the last year under federal funding the school will operate with a staff that can be financed by the district alone. This will be accomplished by trading teaching positions for teacher aides at a ratio of one teacher for three teacher aides. The net result will be that nine of the ten current teacher aide positions and ten of thirteen regular teaching positions will be kept, thus reducing the combined teacher/teacher aide staff from 23 to 19. By redistributing personnel, the school hopes to demonstrate that the project can operate without special funds.

The current dissemination activity is aimed at solving the problem of having a lasting influence among other schools in the district. Area principals and teachers visit the ELC to become acquainted with its work. It is hoped that what the Center is doing will provide encouragement to them for moving toward improved educational programs. The Center does not seek "carbon copies" of its program. It believes each school must develop its own structure for implementing these kinds of ideas. There are numerous organizational and structural patterns which could provide the vehicle for implementing the theories of Project CREATES. Regardless of the organization, curriculum, methodology, or structure, the teacher is still the significant person in the education of the young. How he relates to children and what he does in their presence is still the crucial factor.

Notes

(1) William Glasser. *Schools Without Failure.* (New York: Harper and Row, 1969).
(2) Krevitsky, Nathan I. (Project Director), *The Gift of Heaven,* A Report on Project CREATES, Title III, ESEA 89-10, Tucson Public Schools, District #1, Tucson, Arizona.
(3) *Ibid.*

III

Care and Share— A Program to Reduce Dropouts

James D. Rangles

If you should walk into a "Care and Share" classroom at Ontario (California) High School, students would probably not notice you because they are so engrossed in their schoolwork. Why? There is rarely a student who is not vitally interested in his peers and their opinions of him. Care and Share students are grouped not according to ability, but as a result of their own sociometric choice. There are four or five to a table where they work on the subject matter of the classroom. The subject could be English, mathematics, science or any business course taught at Ontario High School. The assignments do not differ greatly from those given in a conventional class; lectures, recitations, etc., are not ruled out.

There is one noticeable difference, however. On the wall is a chart recording group scores and indicating how each group is performing compared to others in the class. The visitor would find the classroom atmosphere relaxed, but busy and friendly.

The Care and Share program was developed when the incentives for school attendance were systematically analyzed in a research study completed in 1968. (1) This research found that conventional classroom procedures did little to satisfy the "need to belong" felt by many potential dropouts. The responses of dropouts paralleled those found in other studies, especially those of Dr. Donald McNassor of The Claremont Graduate School. (2) In both studies, dropouts expressed little regret at dropping out of school themselves, but felt it would be an unwise act for the average student. To the dropouts, dropping out had some of the inevitability of Greek tragedy. "They had to do their job and I had to do mine." The school system simply was not compatible with what they viewed as important to themselves.

To counteract this feeling of alienation, a number of Ontario High School teachers volunteered to initiate Care and Share procedures in their classrooms. Starting with one teacher in 1968-69, the number has grown to twenty-three. Consequently more than 1,000 of the 1,300 students enrolled at Ontario High School find themselves in one or more Care and Share classes.

Sociometric Grouping

The formation of sociometric groups sounds simple but is actually quite complex. The student is given a numbered list of the students in his class and is asked to rank in the order of his preference those with whom he would like to work. His ten choices of working partners are placed with the choices of his classmates and sent to the Institute for Educational Computing at the nearby Claremont Colleges. There the computer forms student groups from the input of student choices. It aims, within certain limitations, to group those who want to be together.

It is the "certain limitations" that make the problem complex. Popular students tend to pick each other to form an "in group" which would operate to exclude an "out group." The polarities of popularity and unpopularity would occur if the computer used cohesiveness alone as the determiner to place students in a group. Consequently, before the grouping is done, the computer performs the initial step of ranking students in the order of their popularity.

Inasmuch as a student's "high pick" should have more weight than a low one, the first choices are given more "weight" than lower choices in determining where each student's popularity ranks in relation to the rest of the class. The most popular students are separated by making each one a nucleus around which a group is constructed. The number of "leaders" thus set apart is contingent on the number of groups into which the teacher wants a class divided.

For example, if a teacher wants a class of thirty-five students divided into seven groups of five each, the first step would be for the computer to identify the seven most popular students and place one in each group. The second step consists of forming groups of maximum cohesiveness around the popular "leaders." However, once the group is formed the "most popular" student does not always become its leader. The prime consideration for forming groups in this way is not so much to provide group leadership but rather to prevent cliques of very popular students from taking over as the top group in class, leaving less popular students out of contention for recognition.

Preference for a student as a working partner changes from day to day, almost from minute to minute. Those preferences expressed at the beginning of a classroom period may have been radically changed by the end of the period. The shy, quiet student, who formerly was not given much recognition, may in the crucible of goal-oriented group interaction be found to have talent and appeal previously unrecognized. To allow for these dynamic changes in student preference, choices are requested every three weeks and submitted to the computer. The groups are then restructured on the basis of the new choices. At the end of each three-week period the most productive group is given recognition by means of a note sent home to the parents of each member.

Analyzing the Program

The benefits of the program, now in its fourth year, are still being analyzed. Empirical observations from students, counselors, teachers, and parents indicate that student behavior improves and that a new incentive is provided for classroom achievement. The incentive seems to be particularly effective with lower achieving students, and especially with those who have become failure prone and given up in a regular classroom.

In analyzing why the program has grown and been given such wide acceptance by this particular school, the following characteristics appear to carry the most weight:

1) Each student, regardless of his ability, has a chance at being successful. No one starts out feeling he will never have a chance of receiving commendation.
2) Teenagers are anxious to "try their wings" by making choices that are not dictated by adults. They must, however, rise or fall with the results of that choice. This comprises a true learning experience.
3) "It feels good to know you are wanted." Students entering a group know that they are desired by many of their peers in that group.
4) Latent leadership can be developed. No one can practice leadership by himself. He must have the responsibility of a task-oriented group with which he can practice and learn leadership.
5) Success generates success. Even slower students experience the joy of doing their best and finding they can make a contribution that will bring them commendation.
6) Parents appreciate a friendly, complimentary note from the school.
7) Teachers discover that the leaders in the class are not always the ones they would have picked. By following the natural and uncoerced choice of the students, the teacher may examine not only the social structure of the class, but also may observe the dynamic changes which occur.
8) Being a high achiever in a subject does not separate a student from his peers as a "darned average raiser" as conventional grading does. Care and Share makes him a more desirable member of the group and a more profitable companion.

9) Each student comes to be valued for the uniqueness of his particular talent. As group members undertake more complex tasks, such abilities as drawing, acting, organizing, writing, or even being humorous are recognized; students are appreciated for the way they contribute to making this world a happier place and surmounting difficulties more easily.
10) Each student broadens his range of acquaintance. Ethno-social barriers are easily broken in a mutual effort to achieve common goals. (Forty percent of Ontario High School students belong to an ethnic minority.)
11) Discipline problems have decreased as the program has enlarged. After three years of operation 69.7 percent of the total student body were enrolled in one or more Care and Share classes, and 29 percent of the faculty had one or more such class. During the same period the number of discipline cases declined sharply. In the first year of the program (1968-69), the ratio of the number of appearances before the Student Personnel Services Committee for disciplinary reasons to the number of students in the school was 17:2. By 1970-71 this figure had decreased to 11:0, the decrease being largely accounted for by the significantly smaller number of disciplinary appearances of students in Care and Share classes.

Program weaknesses are centered around three areas:

1) Lack of secondary school teacher training in group work theory and practice.
2) Student unfamiliarity with the demands of a new and different system of evaluation.
3) Inertia of a long established and successful system of education to change and meet new demands.

In the early stages of the program, the computer programming appeared to be a nearly insurmountable obstacle. It still remains unavailable to the average school district data center, because of its complexity and cost. New developments in remote terminal inputs to sophisticated computer centers have provided a solution to this problem.

Costs vary, depending upon the cost of installing a remote terminal, and that of providing a typist to collect data, type it into the computer, and distribute the print-outs to teachers. Cost per student, per school year, for one thousand students for this service is roughly $5.47. Cost per student should decline sharply if there were more classes and students utilizing to the full the remote input terminal and its operator. It presently is financed as a part of classroom instruction costs of an ESEA Title I project.

The Care and Share project has been growing by about one-third its size each year since its inception. It would be unrealistic to expect a continuation of this rate of growth because it is difficult to secure teachers familiar with its implementation. It should continue to grow over the foreseeable future, however, especially since the availability of computer technology is increasing.

The future should find us taking more advantage of the computer to add flexibility to a student's range of choice. This should especially be true where his choice must be reconciled to a "choice back" by another person or persons. For example, classes could be chosen and organized contingent on mutual choice involving the teacher and/or students.

Notes

(1) James D. Rangles, "The Chaffey High School Dropout" (Ontario, California: Chaffey Union High School District, 1968). Mimeographed.

(2) Claremont Graduate School and University Center, "The Prodigal Sons—Studies in Identity, Report No. 5" (Claremont, California: Claremont Graduate School and University Center, 1968).

IV

Education in the Newton (Iowa) Community School District

Wilbur R. Smith
and David L. Cronin

Newton is the county seat of Jasper County which is located in the approximate center of Iowa. The Newton Community School District has an enrollment of about 5,000 students housed in eight elementary schools, two junior high schools, and one high school.

Prior to 1969, the educational program was considered quite conservative. At that time, the School Board decided that a set of forward-looking objectives of education, devised in 1966, should be implemented. Among other things, these objectives indicated that Newton schools should provide educational opportunities for the optimum growth of all children; recognize, with variable teaching strategies, that children differ in abilities, capacities, and patterns of growth; and provide opportunities for children to learn how to learn, to master the tools of learning, to explore careers, and to develop initial skills and understandings necessary for them to gain entry into the career area of their choice.

At the opening of the school year in 1969, the superintendent called upon the staff to accept their contractual obligations to implement this district policy, to refashion their teaching strategies where necessary, and work toward the attainment of these goals.

The atmosphere in the district that first year was an agglomeration of conflicting feelings—excitement among those who had hoped for opportunities to be more flexible, frustration among those who were comfortable in their settled ways, a certain degree of chaos which comes with abrupt change, and some confused parents who were hearing complaints from anxious teachers at teacher-parent conferences, in the beauty parlor, barbershop, and marketplace, and at social gatherings.

One of the greatest problems was confusion over terminology. Individualized instruction was interpreted as every child having to be instructed individually, and everyone doing something different. "How is this possible?" asked teachers and parents. "Each child going at his own rate" was interpreted as each child deciding when and how he wants to learn, and if he decides to do nothing, that too is all right. Providing opportunities to work independently in order to help the child learn how to learn was interpreted as each child having to figure out everything by himself. "The teacher is no longer teaching," proclaimed some parents.

Several procedures were adopted to offset this concern. A ten-week, on-site seminar for teachers and principals was held during the winter. It was designed to build background and help teachers improve techniques. Teachers and principals were encouraged to visit other schools within and outside Iowa. Consultants were invited to spend a day or two visiting schools and meeting with teachers.

Despite resistance, the Newton program began to reflect the proposed objectives. If one had taken a poll in June of 1970, staff support for implementing the concepts embodied within the objectives might have been marginal. However, in April, 1972, following the defeat of a bond issue, the Newton Community Education Association (NCEA) decided to assess teacher support of the program.

The NCEA survey revealed that 83 percent of the faculty were convinced of the validity of this approach. Many positive remarks were offered. Perhaps the most poignant one was: "Trying to teach according to the methods of 25-50 years ago, as some would advocate, would be a step backwards." The survey also indicated that training is still needed for many teachers. One negative respondent wrote: "Many of us are not trained or equipped to teach under the philosophy of individualized instruction."

Just what was transpired in Newton which has increased flexibility in the schools and generated this ferment?

In almost every classroom, one will find students working on different materials or at different levels on the same materials. Often different age children are working together. This is not too unusual at the elementary level, but at Newton this situation exists in most junior and senior high school classes as well. The biology teachers, for example, have organized their program into units with varying degrees of difficulty. Specific behavioral objectives proceed each unit. Students take pre-tests and then set realistic goals for themselves which they pursue at varying rates. An audio-tutorial system has been devised and installed by the teachers for students who can learn best in this way. In 1972, three of the advanced biology students won top state honors for their research projects. One student was selected to present his work at two national contests.

The sophomore writing program has been developed along similar lines. At the opening of the school year, students were given diagnostic tests to assess their differential writing abilities. This led the team, which consists of the entire English faculty, to engage students in work on several different writing tasks such as sentence structure, paragraph construction, separating fact from opinion, expository writing, and poetry. Students speak intelligently about what they are doing and why. In addition, the entire high school English program has been organized into semester-length courses to give students options in meeting the high school English requirement. The attitude of most students toward required English has changed from rejection to mild enthusiasm.

Space does not permit a full description of what is now taking place in the Newton schools. Suffice it to say that it is possible to see, in one or more of the eleven schools, examples of all of the fourteen categories of procedures designed to achieve flexibility which are listed in Appendix A.

It would be presumptuous to predict that the Newton Schools will continue to add procedures and become even more flexible. Many parents are calling for evidence which shows that what is now being done in the classroom is better than the program they experienced. As might be expected, they are using criteria derived from their experience to assess the quality of the program.

One of these criteria is performance on the Iowa Tests of Basic Skills. Since 1969, no progress has been made in these scores. The 1969 composite mean grade equivalent for fourth grade was 5.5. In 1970, it was 4.4; in 1971, 4.5; in 1972, 4.3. Scores in the specific areas of the test reflect this same stable but slight downward trend. Historically, arithmetic achievement, expressed in terms of mean grade equivalents, has been lower than in other areas. Moreover, for children in grade eight, the mean grade equivalent value (7.9) falls slightly below the norm.

In comparing the Newton educational program with that of schools located in smaller towns and rural areas where the scores on the Iowa Basic Skills Tests are usually higher, it is apparent that Newton children enjoy a more diverse learning program. This diversity does cause Newton children to devote less time to instruction in the basic skills, especially as they progress from the primary to upper elementary levels. For example, primary students spend 40 percent of their time in reading instruction, whereas children in grades 4-6 spend only 19 percent.

At this writing the School Board continues to support the Objectives of Education. They realize that those who are demanding a return to the old ways of doing things are members of an adult population having great difficulties living and working together in the complex society of 1972. The objectives currently in force in the Newton schools demand an educational program which should provide young people with better preparation for dealing with the difficult social, emotional, and political problems of our world.

To reconcile the two conflicting forces, district staff is now searching for ways to adjust priorities and programs to correct deficiencies and to preserve the good things which have been created. At the same time a search is underway for methods of assessing outcomes other than the basic skills.

To move forward in this second effort, Newton has begun work on establishing a cost-analysis baseline which will be used for a long-range accountability framework. By June, 1972, it will be known exactly how much time is devoted to each instructional area and how much each student-teacher contact hour costs. The summer of 1972 will be devoted to designing the accountability framework. Hopefully, Newton will find it possible to continue pursuing its overriding goal: "A student-centered approach to education which provides opportunities for each child to attain his full educational development."

A Unique Secondary Program

Newton represents an unusual mix of a manufacturing community located in a predominantly agricultural state. This, plus the commitment of the educational community to meet the learning needs of all individuals, has encouraged the development of different approaches to education within the district. One approach is the School Without Walls (SWW) project. In this program, local business, industry, and service-oriented enterprises collaborate with the SWW staff to develop and carry out instructional units or learning experiences for the individual or small groups of students. It has been SWW's experience that the group size should be limited to about five to provide maximum opportunity for the participants. Learning experiences are provided by experts from the business or industry, usually at the location of the activity. In this way, participants are exposed to the career field of their choice on a first-hand basis by the person who does this work for a living.

The history of the Newton SWW goes back to December, 1969. Following discussions with local business and industrial leaders, a meeting was held at which Dr. John Naisbitt, President of the Urban Research Corporation, presented the concepts underlying the work at Metro High School in Chicago. (1) In September of 1970, an advisory committee of businessmen, industrialists, and other interested persons was appointed to assist in the preliminary planning necessary and in getting the program underway. In November, a Special Needs grant of federal funds was awarded by the State of Iowa Department of Public Instruction. From January, 1971, to

June, 1971, the program was tried on a limited basis. Experience from this initial pilot endeavor provided the background to design and implement the program that is currently in its first full year of operation.

Several objectives were formulated for the program. Without stating these in detail, they are directed toward three related concerns:

1) Preparing for careers: exploration, knowledge about, and initial hands-on skill development.
2) Enlarging the breadth of the high school curriculum available to all students.
3) Increasing the relevancy of courses and the alternatives available so that the programs will be more attractive to the potential dropout and may encourage the return of actual dropouts.

These objectives, plus the current SWW program, are providing the basis for a district-wide career education program. Community resources are being used extensively to meet these objectives. The SWW has already demonstrated its effectiveness as a coordinating agent to bring the potential community resources into contact with students who are seeking relevant learnings in specific career areas. The SWW also helps develop learning experiences to be offered in the community establishments that will create enthusiasm in both student and sponsor. Three examples will illustrate how SWW works:

The United Telephone Company collaborated with the SWW to develop and implement an intensive and successful program. United's course covered seven sessions, with each session ranging from two to three hours in length. Students were selected on the basis of expressed interest.

Sessions took place on the company premises. One session dealt with the operators' jobs; the students helped monitor the handling of toll calls by operators. Another session dealt with construction and maintenance. The class was held at the warehouse where the men who worked there served as instructors. They helped the students set a pole, splice and close a cable, and then demonstrated how the cable functions. All sessions were conducted by employees from the department concerned. For the seventh and final session, the students selected one of the previous six areas and spent up to three more hours working side by side with an expert craftsman.

Another example took place at the Parsons Company, a heavy equipment manufacturing firm. This program consisted of eight sessions of from one and a half to two and a half hours in length. The sessions began with such topics as the philosophy of the company and the overall manufacturing process. Students were then given "hands on" work experience in the various departments such as welding and machine shop. One of the highlights of this program occured when students were taken to the test range and actually operated some of the equipment they had helped to manufacture.

SWW also provides individual opportunities. An excellent example of an experience tailored for an individual need was that of a young man who indicated a strong interest in the legal profession. A local attorney arranged for the student to spend two and one-half full days with him as he tried a case. The student was briefed on the proceedings. He was allowed to sit next to the attorney as he defended his client, and he was with the attorney as the verdict was read. During this experience, the student received considerable counseling from this expert attorney as to schooling and personal requirements needed to enter the legal profession.

These are a few of the many types of learning experiences arranged by SWW. Semi-technical, technical, as well as professional areas are explored. The initial response to the learning experiences has been highly positive. Sponsors have been more than willing to cooperate and have expressed an overwhelmingly enthusiastic reaction to their experiences with the students. Student response has been equally positive. It appears that once a student commits himself to a program in which he is interested, the enthusiasm to carry through remains high. As a result, collaboration between school and community has increased tremendously. Evaluation of the programs carried on thus far indicates that the concept is viable and that it should be expanded. At this writing, approximately 225 students and 100 sponsors have been involved.

SWW programs are available to both full-time students in the conventional school and students who have interrupted their formal education. Students who might be considered dropouts are of especial interest to SWW staff who are designing special programs to encourage them to meet the requirements for graduation. These students are invited to enroll in SWW courses as an alternative to attending the regular high school classes. In addition to becoming involved in the career related activities of SWW, they also resume other learnings under the direction of SWW staff to fulfill requirements for the high school diploma.

These SWW programs for students who are not academically talented or who, for some reason, have rejected the conventional school, operate on a tasks-accomplished basis rather than a time-put-in basis. Students have certain contractual obligations to meet to fulfill requirements. Once these contracts are met, regardless of the time involved, credit is awarded. "Semesters" end when the student fulfills the requirements and is ready to begin a new program. Some students have found it possible to complete a semester's course in nine weeks. Other students take the full 18 weeks, while still others take even more time.

Each day, SWW staff add programs to provide learning experiences about careers and entry into these careers for students.

Procedures are being refined to make all learning experiences as meaningful as possible. It is hoped that additional funding will become available to improve the specialized programs for meeting academic requirements. We also hope to obtain a facility to provide a true learning laboratory for those students who are fulfilling basic requirements. A tutorial arrangement with teachers has already been established to give students the special help needed in learning specialized skills.

As we look to the future, School Without Walls staff want every Newton High School student to become involved in the program. They are convinced that, in addition to the rich academic preparedness a student can already receive, he should also know about the world of work and have an opportunity to work for pay and to work for learning. We eventually see a student beginning career investigation at an early age, building a career profile during the early secondary period, and finally culminating with on-the-job experiences for learning, and on-the-job experiences for pay. In this way, students can be made ready to enter the society as we know it today, and as we foresee it in the future.

Note

(1) See Edgar G. Epps, "Chicago's School Without Walls: The Chicago Public High School for Metropolitan Studies," in Daniel U. Levine, ed., *Models for Integrated Education,* (Worthington, Ohio: Charles A. Jones Publishing Co., 1971), pp. 32-42.

Humane Alternative Schools

Don Glines

Philosophic Overview

Humaneness, alternatives, options, both personalized and individualized, are the key concepts for providing the flexibility necessary to achieve significant improvement in the educational institutions of the United States during the decade of the 70's. The operating procedures of many schools, school districts, and colleges over the past years have rarely resembled humane centers for learning opportunities.

Recently, however, a growing number of individuals, schools, and even a few school districts and colleges have made commitments to reform by piloting creative programs for learners built upon those key concepts of personal, humane, alternatives. The Wilson Campus School and the newly developing School of Educational Alternatives at Mankato State College, Mankato, Minnesota, are two such efforts. Wilson is a pre-kindergarten through traditional grade 12 school of approximately 600 students, noted the past four years for its pioneering efforts in innovative approaches. The college component of this development is designed to prepare teachers to work in open, Wilson type schools. As this latter attempt is just in its beginning stages, the description here is limited to the program which has been in operation at Wilson. Though it is in a college laboratory setting, Wilson has been conducted as a public school, so that things learned can be implemented in a practical setting in any school district in the United States, if the leadership of that school community is committed to creating options for individual differences and alternative learning preferences.

For proof that rapid, dramatic, massive change is possible in school systems, a brief description of Wilson in July, 1968, is essential. At that time, Wilson could best be described as a good, conventional school. The building was of the traditional egg crate design; allocated staff and budget were average for Minnesota; the students were typical representatives of a large, rural, midwestern community. They scored above average on the traditional national tests; those who went on to college succeeded as well as students from most schools. The parents were generally satisfied, and the staff included both extremes of quality—very strong and very weak.

The elementary division had nothing but self-contained rooms; the high school followed a rigid, 55-minute period, 1,2,3 type schedule with the usual A, B, C, D, F report cards. All seventh grade students were required to take English, social studies, math, science, physical education, and a semester each of art and music. Rooms were arranged with 30 desks facing the blackboard; dress codes, hourly attendance, excuse notes from home, bells, study halls, and hall passes were part of the policies. Single textbooks were assigned for the various courses; athletic eligibility rules were based upon report cards. Special education students were placed in one of the "boxes" with the teacher for the mentally retarded. Reading and language arts were taught from 9:00-10:15 each morning. The school was in a neighborhood attendance area. In other words, Wilson was trapped by all the ritual and ceremony that still clutters most schools in the United States.

The two-month period from July to September, 1968, witnessed tremendous change. Complete transformations were made in all aspects of the school. On-going innovation has continued over the past four years. Wilson is not the best school in the nation; it is not a model to copy. But its evolution does represent a realistic story of what can take place when a staff adopts a philosophy which incorporates this basic assemption: "if schools are to be significantly better, they must be significantly different."

Program Description

Schools described as being innovative have adopted one or more procedures to achieve change and flexibility. Most of these are discussed in Chapter I of this book. Wilson found that no single approach is sufficient; instead, all of them must be interwoven. Six major components of the school were identified: philosophy, learning preferences, curriculum, organization, facilities, and evaluation. Nine to twelve sub-listings were listed under each component, or a total of 69 identified changes needed to achieve the flexibility desired. Not one of the six components could be omitted. If one of the 69 changes were ignored, the other 68 did not work as well. This multi-factored interrelated concept led to a most flexible school environment. Some of the 69 changes are briefly discussed here in an attempt to describe the program in operation in January, 1972. (1)

Probably the one facet of the present Wilson effort that really makes a difference is the person-to-person emphasis. Without a doubt, the real changes in the school revolve around human relationships, not around scheduling, carpeting, team teaching, or individualized instruction.

At Wilson, students select their own teachers-facilitators-partners in learning. There is little difference between students and teachers; rather the relationship is described as people helping people learn. No student is ever assigned to a teacher or reverse. Six factors are crucial in attaining this person match: personality, perception, age, sex, interest, skill. How many principals or computers or teachers in most schools sit down to determine whether 6-year-old Billy needs an attractive young woman in a short skirt, a grandma, a daddy, or a combination of these, at this moment in his life?

Youngsters no longer sign up for courses; in fact, there are no courses to select. Instead they find people with whom they would like to learn in an interrelated fashion. After they have been involved in a meaningful learning experience, they give their involvement a "title" to record on their experience sheet. This means that there are no required courses, K-12. Wilson is completely nongraded; 6-year-olds are often working together with 18-year-olds. The younger folk generally have the same choices and alternatives available to older individuals.

The students further select their own advisor-counselor. Each adult becomes a warm, empathetic friend to those youngsters who have selected that individual for guidance and a close, personal relationship. There are none of the one counselor to 300 students ratios. These practices, which so obviously rely on people for successful implementation, soon led to the realization that the affective domain was the real key to success in any school, especially one attempting to be open and flexible. Self-image, success, peer and adult relationships, family considerations became the crucial issues.

Closely on the heels of the affective area, especially for the younger persons, comes the psychomotor. That is why physical education, industrial arts, and home economics, and then music and art are the most important areas for primary age children. The cognitive is still important, but only after, or at the same time, that assurances are available that the affective and psychomotor are in good shape. There is no problem in learning reading and math skills, for example, if the affective and motor areas are strong. But all the reading instruction in the world doesn't help if the affective area isn't solved before or in conjunction with the cognitive tasks. This is why personalized programming for each student is practiced at Wilson. Group requirements are impossible when students are given personal attention.

As programs became personalized, it was apparent that individual learning preferences demanded individualized learning methods. About 80 percent of an individual's time at Wilson is spent in one-to-one conferences with an adult and/or in informal self-developed groupings of students, in independent study, and in open lab. About 20 percent of the day is spent in small groups of five or six, generally the biggest "class" at Wilson. On occasions, common thread large groups are conducted on topics of interest. The first three years these combinations were arranged through a "daily smorgasbord" operation; each day a brand new master schedule was constructed. This fourth year the school is piloting an "unseen schedule." Students arrange meeting times with other staff and students as business people arrange conferences—by appointments as necessary. There is no longer a master schedule built in the office or by teams at Wilson.

In this type of philosophy, optional attendance to both school and "classes" became a must, as did a completely open campus for all students. Students were trusted and adopted a slogan of "with freedom goes responsibility and courtesy." Staff members have the same degrees of freedom. Obviously dress codes, bells, notes from home, and all the rest were eliminated.

The school operates on a twelve-month clock; students may drop in, drop out, speed up, slow down, start, stop whenever they wish. There are no quarters, semesters, or end of the year. Students may vacation whenever they wish. The same program is offered in July and January. All day food service is available for there are some who feel that the "protein nibblers" should eat six meals a day.

There are no graduation requirements from high school. A student may take four years of "basket weaving." Diplomas are awarded through individual evaluations, not group requirements. There are no report cards; even seniors get no class rank, grade point average, credits, or other standard evaluations; yet they are accepted in the colleges and universities.

To provide more flexibility, students select one of four options to follow as guidelines toward their learning activities. The free option gives students tremendous leeway; the open option provides freedom, but with more evaluation; the planned option is a similar approach but guarantees more guidance; the closed option provides more structure. These options are selected during a conference which includes both parents, the child, and the advisor. They can be altered whenever desired.

Differentiated staffing, three nights a week for a lighted school, efforts to truly interrelate curricula through three teams (Studios for Evolving Persons, Studios for Emerging Environments, and Studios for Future Media), unpaid social service, human relations curricula, person-to-person type learning experiences, remodeled facilities, student exchanges to Mexico and Indian reservations, a school without walls, programs for 3- and 4-year-olds, and many other such concepts are involved at Wilson as part of the massive changes necessary to achieve true flexibility in the school.

Evaluation Efforts

The program described above has been functioning well for four years. Total systematic efforts at evaluation have been sporadic, but have followed three definite approaches: individual students, total school evaluation, and national accountability.

In the area of individual student evaluation, comparative grades and tests have been eliminated; instead all students set their personal goals in conferences with the adults whom they have selected. Progress toward these goals is evaluated, again in one-to-one conferences. Five copies of the goal sheets or progress reports are now used: a preliminary goal sheet which is sent to the advisor as soon as the youngster makes a commitment to learn in a given program, and then four follow-up copies, one of which goes to the student and parent, one to the adults with whom he is learning, one to the advisor, and one to the office where completed experiences are recorded on the Experience Record.

These reports have a space for goals, for accomplishments and adjustments, and for various comments. In addition to this report, there is an advisor evaluation sheet which is a subjective judgment of the individual's yearly growth in the affective, psychomotor, and cognitive domains, as well as a look at the future. Through these efforts, the staff is satisfied that meaningful learning and worthwhile student experiences are being obtained through the current program. Discipline problems as commonly described in most schools have been almost entirely eliminated. Stealing and use of drugs still occur, but even these are minimal; an acceptance of responsibility in the open school and close personal relationships are apparently the major ingredients for solving most of the routine disciplinary cases.

In the area of total school evaluation, Wilson has participated in studies to compare students at Wilson with those in more conventional settings. Wilson does not believe in group use of such tests as the Iowa Basic Skills, I.Q.'s, and various other achievement batteries. However, the school has cooperated in studies in an effort to reach some conclusions based upon more conventional ratings than their own.

In the area of the cognitive domain, Wilson has held its own. Test scores are about the same as in schools using more conventional approaches to learning. Unfortunately, those tests do not measure many of the cognitive knowledges felt important at Wilson. However, in the affective domain, Wilson students have scored significantly better in surveys of self-image, and of their attitude toward school. In other words, their norm indicates that generally they like themselves and their school better than students in more conventional programs do. In the psychomotor areas, the test results and comparative studies are inconclusive, although subjective analysis is very positive toward the Wilson approach, especially for young children.

With regard to national accountability efforts, Wilson is more concerned with self-direction, responsibility, decision-making, self-image, success: in other words, the affective domain. Then the program is aimed at the important motor skills. The staff challenges the "experts" to help develop measurements for these areas. When they do, Wilson will be happy to be "accountable," even in the cognitive, but the cognitive must include knowledge of all areas, not just language arts, math, and social studies. The school feels that content in industrial arts is just as important as math.

Wilson is one of the few schools with a full-time research coordinator. Over twenty studies at the master's thesis level are currently underway in the building. More effort is going into the evaluation of Wilson than most public schools. No conclusive "proof" is available yet, but from what evidence there is, and from subjective staff evaluation, after four years there is no indication that the school is headed in the wrong direction; most guidelines point to continued innovations within the same general philosophic stance.

Problem Areas

The first three sections of this paper were positive in their conclusions that the Wilson program has been a success to date. There is no doubt that at this moment in time, the positives by far overshadow any negatives. However, no attempt is intended to hide the fact that there have been and still are problems. The greatest difficulty, and one which remains, is that of quality staff. Wherever there are excellent teachers, there are excellent programs. The great adult at Wilson is the one who is that warm, empathetic body, who uses the indirect approach, and who has a good interrelated cognitive background. But the real key is that wonderful, lovable, love-argue-kill-and-make-up relationship with kids. Youngsters just flock to those areas with that type of person. The experience with students selecting their own teacher, advisors, and courses is convincing that tenure laws must be changed to provide easier dismissal of those who don't fit, or at least easier transfer to schools and programs to match their teaching preferences.

Wilson had to take the existing staff, building, students, and budget with no inservice training, no consultants, and, in two months' time, do a complete about-face. In the succeeding three years, the great teachers have become really great, the middle have improved, but the weaker teachers have settled further toward the bottom. Unfortunately, personality conflicts still exist between staff members. Teacher A can work with teacher B and teacher C, but B and C continue to tangle. Slow progress is being made in this area, even after "human relations" sessions.

Another problem came from a small portion of the community—namely from a minority of the college faculty, and a group of parents who felt they had lost control of "their" school. Both groups generally opposed the director on basic differences in personality and philosophy. The second year a petition was circulated to have the director removed and the school returned to "sanity." This problem was met head-on by a group of "for" parents and students who developed a counter-petition greater than the "against." Then an open meeting of a combination of large and small groups was held for four hours one evening to air concerns. Further, it was made quite clear that there would be at least one alternative school in Mankato, and those not liking the program could transfer to a more structured school in the city. The director remained and the program flourished.

Finance and maintenance areas, as in most places, were problems. The school operates at about the 50th percentile in terms of costs of schools in Minnesota. During the second year of this past four-year program, a special "catch up" fund was provided to buy badly needed library books, tapes, carrels, some carpet, and classroom materials. The other three years the school has operated on the conventional budget. In fact, this year a 25 percent cut occurred because of a drop in college enrollments. Thus Wilson has less money this year for daily operation than in its last year (1967-68) as a traditional program. The school is operated primarily through allocations from the state legislature, although state aid funds and additional money from the local school district are provided.

All funds are state tax dollars. There are no federal grants or other special reimbursements. The key is not more money, but in reallocating resources. Schools must take their current budgets and use them differently. That is how Wilson has provided more financial flexibility on the same budget allocations as for a conventional school. Staff was increased, for example, at no additional total cost through differentiated staffing.

Care of equipment is always a problem; students have been exceptionally good about not taking materials that are left on open shelves for them to use. However, over the four years the school has lost a few cassettes, wasted some art supplies, and had some damage to equipment by the usual few. As a result, Wilson is moving from a very liberal help-yourself policy on supplies to a more middle-of-the-road approach. In teaming, too, it became necessary to assign teams to the care of certain areas of the building. Some rooms, such as the auditorium, became "nobody's room," and thus damage occurred. Now each of the studios has responsibility for a portion of the building.

A last, unusual problem has been lack of student and parent involvement groups. They seem to be so content with the personalized approach to their learning, and with their ability to have immediate personal contact when there appears to be a problem, that student/parent advisory groups, councils, and other such efforts have failed. It is difficult to know how the "group" feels, as there are no representative groups. Group consensus can only be inferred from individual contacts.

Future Directions

The Wilson pilot is just one small but extremely meaningful experience to help indicate the future direction of education during this decade. If the United States is built upon such concepts as freedom, democracy, tolerance, justice, and humaneness, then certainly one of the key values in the entire society is one of the major concepts that school districts have failed to accept—the meaning of alternatives.

The neighborhood, required attendance area school, required courses, assigned rooms and teachers, A, B, C report cards, and all other such procedures represent a monopoly. Every school district has the obligation to offer each child, parent, and teacher the opportunity to live in an open, flexible school, a semi-flexible school, or a more structured school, the final choice being dependent upon personal learning and life preferences. The district that forces all students into one neighborhood school which is basically the same for everyone is guilty of perpetuating a major tragedy.

Whatever the method, every district must offer each student humane choices. The great districts of the 70's will provide these alternatives. Wilson type schools are more than worth the effort for the benefits derived by those who select the open approach. Wilson is not a free school; it is another alternative which districts should provide as a mini-program.

The fact that officials at Mankato State view the four-year effort at Wilson as successful is indicated in the decision to start, in the spring of 1972, the School of Educational Alternatives. This will be a four-year college program to prepare teachers for flexible schools.

The successful Wilson student and teacher, in spite of all the problems and frustrations, would never turn back the clock; none want to return to the bell ringing, hall pass, group-paced instruction, A, B, C, D, F type procedures which existed at Wilson Campus School prior to July, 1968. Instead, all eyes are turned toward the exciting potential which challenges discovery in the future.

Note

(1) A more complete description of Wilson is available in Don Glines, *Creating Humane Schools* (Mankato, Minnesota: Campus Publishers, 1971).

VI

An Open Elementary School

Robert J. Ross

The Paul A. Smith Elementary School, located in Franklin, New Hampshire, is a school of open design with a nongraded organization involving team teaching and individualized instruction. Its basic purpose is to enable each pupil to experience success and to progress at his own rate of learning.

This basic goal is further expanded in our stated philosophy:

> Education is a continuous process of growth. Therefore, the school should be continually concerned with the physical, emotional, social, and intellectual growth and development of the student as an individual. It should provide an opportunity for participation in a wide variety of student activities to enable the student to become a secure, responsible member of society.

We are offering children the opportunity to progress at their own learning rate—a pace slow enough for the slowest children and fast enough for the most advanced student. Slow children should not be frustrated by being forced to reach for levels of achievement that are impossible for them to reach. Bright children should not be bored by the unnecessary repetition that causes lack of interest.

We are attempting to develop a child whose attitude toward learning has as its roots self-motivation, not a child whose sole motivation is the grade he may obtain or the pleasure he will bring his teacher and parents. We want to create the child who desires to learn because he finds learning enjoyable, creative, and self-satisfying. We want children to be self-directed and self-disciplined.

To implement this philosophy, we are individualizing our program to fit the needs of small groups of children with the ultimate aim to design a program for each child.

The Beginning

Franklin is a small, industrial community located in central New Hampshire with a population of 7,000 and a school population of 1,775 public school children and 231 parochial school children. Faced with the need for additional school space, Superintendent Herman N. Donegan and the school committee, decided to build a new elementary school in the Lawndale section of Ward 1, an area where the neighborhood school was discontinued in 1957.

During the first meeting, the building committee, composed of eight local citizens, four appointed by the school committee and four appointed by the city council, discussed building a traditional school or the possibility of looking to new ideas in school building. The film "How to Build a School House" was shown to the building committee. This forward-looking film had much to do with the decision to examine new building concepts before proceeding further with their thinking.

The Educational Facilities Laboratory located in New York City offered to help us explore new ideas by underwriting a visit to a number of experimental schools in several states. Making the trip were Superintendent Donegan, the chairman of the school board, and an architect assigned to the building committee. The group reported to the building committee at the next meeting and suggested that the entire committee visit innovative plants. With the interest generated from the film and the trip, the committee as a whole decided to visit the Horace Mann School in Lexington, Massachusetts, and the Timberlane School located in Plaistow, New Hampshire. Following these trips, the committee committed themselves to the type of building that looked to the future.

With this commitment, it immediately became important that an inservice training program for the staff be provided to make the instruction effective in this new setting. The effectiveness of operation of the schools visited in New York, Illinois, and Missouri appeared to be in proportion to their preplanning.

The New Hampshire State Department of Education and Plymouth State College were approached and agreed to assist in arranging and conducting an inservice training program to operate concurrently with the building committee's planning and construction of an open-type school.

Teacher involvement in the organizational pattern and curriculum development of the new school began before the contract for the building was awarded. An initial phase of this program was the sending of the elementary principal to a workshop on nongrading and team teaching.

In the spring of 1967, interested teachers visited schools in Lexington, Amherst, Winchester, and Woodbury, Massachusetts. A staff survey following the visitation period favored further study of the concepts involving nongrading and team teaching. During the fall of 1967, an Institute on Team Teaching and Individualized Instruction was taught in Franklin under the sponsorship of Plymouth State College. The Institute was financed through a $3,000 grant obtained from the Educational Facilities Laboratory.

Operating concurrently with the Institute, the volunteer staff was released from their regular classroom duties to meet monthly with consultants. These meetings were supported by the Center of Educational Field Studies, University of New Hampshire. The follow-up program for the preschool planning sessions was a 1968 summer workshop focused on curriculum development and financed by ESEA, Title I.

The Present

The Paul A. Smith School has a population of approximately 320 children. The staff consists of a principal, ten teachers, four teachers' aides, two clerks and part-time personnel consisting of a nurse, librarian, art and music teachers. With the exception of the kindergarten, which is a self-contained room, the instructional areas, including the resource center, are completely open with no interior walls or partitions. Four teacher stations are located on one end of a rectangular building and a six-teacher area is located on the opposite end. The resource center separates the two areas.

The open classroom lends itself to two important concepts: mobility of children and communication between teachers. Children may move from one group to another as they are distributed and redistributed through the various flexible levels of learning. Groups as large as 70 or as small as desirable may be readily organized for instruction. Teachers are continually in communication with one another. Inasmuch as the correct placement of children demands a high degree of teacher interaction, this communication is the backbone of team effort.

The Smith School is a unique blend of federal and state financed projects, staff commitment and team cooperation among community, school board, state education department and colleges. Two of our most important state-federal projects are labeled SOLVE—*S*upport for *O*pen concept *L*earning areas through *V*aried *E*ducational teams, and PRIDE—*P*rogram for *R*etardate *I*ntegration through *D*evelopmental *E*ducation.

SOLVE is the cooperative effort of six school districts operating open concept schools located in different areas of New Hampshire. The project is financed by a Title III grant. The emphasis is on the individual learner with several concentrations: curriculum development, teacher decision-making, use of teacher aides as educational facilitators, diagnosis of each individual, and the use of materials to prescribe an effective strategy for learning. Franklin receives approximately $20,000 in direct and indirect financial assistance.

Formerly, our educable mentally retarded (EMR) youngsters and those with emotional disturbances and physical handicaps were segregated in one room. They remained with the same teacher for six years. This segregation reinforced the image in these children that they are not only different, but also they should not associate with other children. It fostered an extremely low tolerance level from other students. Project PRIDE's philosophy is that educable mentally retarded children, when properly diagnosed, can achieve their maximum capabilities in a typical classroom setting. We feel this can be achieved to a greater degree by integrating these children in an open school setting on a partial, half-time or full-time basis, depending upon the readiness of the individual child. The security of identification with their "home base" teacher is always available to them.

Support for our integration process came recently from research conducted by Dr. Jay Gottlieb, Educational Evaluator for the Research Institute for Educational Problems, Cambridge, Massachusetts. It was found that, on the basis of sociometric investigations, the retarded child in the Paul Smith School was socially accepted to a lesser degree than the nonretarded child. Nevertheless, in comparison to retarded children elsewhere, the EMR children in the Smith School occupied a far more favorable social position because they are rejected less often.

The Smith School has a primary and an intermediate team, each composed of four teachers, an aide and a clerk with approximately 130 youngsters. In addition, there is a kindergarten and a special class consisting of children who have learning disabilities, taught by an instructor and two aides.

Art, music, physical education and library are scheduled in a block of time. Because these areas are taught by personnel outside the teams, teachers are provided with two hours of planning time. Combined team planning takes place on Thursday afternoon from 1:00 p.m. to 4:00 p.m. The school schedule calls for a six-hour school day (8:30 a.m. to 12 and 12:45 to 3:15 p.m.) on every day except Thursday. Thursday consists of three and one half hours of instruction and three hours of team planning. Children are dismissed at the conclusion of the lunch period. By starting one-half hour earlier each morning, the children at the Smith School are not deprived of any instructional time. The three-hour total team planning period provides a realistic work period for continuous long- and short-range planning. Total team planning discourages a curriculum gap that might appear between the primary and intermediate units. Moreover, it encourages a continuous flow of children from the primary to the intermediate and from the intermediate to primary units.

Morning classes usually consist of instruction in the language arts and math units, while the afternoon instruction is in the areas of science and social studies. Instructional times are scheduled in blocks and are flexible to take advantage of the need to group and regroup children.

Children are grouped in language arts based on their performance in the communicative skills of reading, writing, listening, and speaking. A basic language arts continuum has been developed for the primary levels. Skills have identified and listed in sequential order and placed on McBee Retrieval Cards. Materials from several publishers are used at both the primary and intermediate levels.

A grammar continuum has been developed for the intermediate section. The program uses placement tests to determine the areas in which the child should start to work and pre-tests to determine the skills the child needs to master. Self-teaching learning packs are used to aid the child in acquiring the skills and post-tests measure mastery of a given skill.

Mathematics is quite highly individualized. We are using the Individually Prescribed Instruction program which has been developed by the Research and Development Center at the University of Pittsburgh and is disseminated by Research for Better Schools located in Philadelphia, Pennsylvania.

The mathematics program consists of eight levels (A-H). Each level consists of skills written in measurable behavioral outcomes ordered sequentially. Youngsters progress through these levels at their own pace, each child working on his specific mathematics needs. Teachers with 33 children have 33 math programs operating at the same time. The program allows a child to master skills in which he has demonstrated a deficiency. He is not expected to practice or work in areas in which he is already proficient. Initially, each child is given a placement test to locate his approximate level in each mathematics area. After placement is determined, the child begins to work at his lowest level of performance. The student takes a pre-test on the skills taught in each progressive unit and then works on the skills in which he is having difficulty. Work continues on each skill until mastery is attained as measured by post-tests.

The primary teachers identified topics to be taught in social studies. Intermediate teachers developed a four-part social studies program. The parts include: values (how to develop friendships, acquiring a more positive attitude toward one's classmates, school, adults, etc.), two levels of map and globe skills, and a content course using a cultural-anthropological format. Children progress through each of the four social studies areas during the school year.

Through Project SOLVE we have acquired materials from the Webster/McGraw-Hill series, *Experiences in Science*. This is an experience-centered program, rather than a book-centered or demonstration-type approach. It builds upon the child's natural curiosity, encouraging him to discover fascinating, scientific facts for himself. The child is provided with the laboratory equipment he needs to perform his own experiments.

Unit topics in the natural and physical sciences have been selected. Learning packs have been developed which allow a child to pursue a given scientific topic in an independent manner. During the school year, the students progress through topics in natural science and physical science, and then return to natural science. Natural science study in the fall and spring takes advantage of plant life and natural phenomena available at those times.

In June, 1971, we completed a three-year evaluation of our total program. The evaluation includes a tabulation of the results of the Stanford Achievement Test for the past four years, student and teacher surveys of attitudes and reactions, a parent reaction survey, as well as a summary of comments recorded by the numerous visitors to our school.

Our initial evaluation supports the fact that we have created an environment where children sense a new freedom to learn in an informal, nonthreatening manner, where a child may progress at a learning pace best suited for himself as an individual. This environment stimulates a child to express his true feelings and has made him more sensitive toward the feelings of others. The Stanford Test results indicate that we have accomplished this without any loss in the academic achievement of our youngsters.

Our new, individualized reporting system to parents is now more consistent with our total program. Multi-cards allow the teacher and/or parents to select the best combination to meet the child's needs. There is no single time for reporting the progress of all youngsters. One student's progress might be reported six or more times a year, while the progress of another might be reported a minimum of three times. This reporting system is experimental. Revision and updating will be done at the conclusion of the 1971-72 as well as the 1972-73 school years.

Work habits and attitudes are self-evaluated by the child and rated by the teacher. This process may be accomplished in a joint conference or done separately and the results compared at a later time. Teacher-parent conferences are still an important part of our reporting system. While we do not schedule selective days for such conferences, the process is continuous and arrangements may be made by the teacher to see the parents at school or at their home.

Problems

What are some of the problems to be faced in the operation of an open concept school? Recruiting and training teachers to work together as a team is essential. If anything, the teachers' role is more arduous in these schools. The open-space school requires teachers who are capable of relating to their peers and of structuring an individualized learning environment that enhances diversity of interactions, fosters independent thinking and creates a zest for learning. Training of personnel for the Smith School has been aided by our inservice workshops and our student teaching program.

Lack of individual materials and equipment necessary to supplement the curriculum is a realistic concern. Federal projects and redirecting the use of local funds can help solve this problem.

Public support must be developed whenever one undertakes an innovative program. This calls for a sound public relations program involving radio and television, newsletters to parents, material for the newspapers, and speaking engagements at local organizations.

The orientation of students is an important consideration in the operation of an open concept school. Children must be given the opportunity to be responsible for their own behavior. They must be taught how to work with one another. At the same time, there must be a balance between self-directed and teacher-directed activities so that we do not neglect direct teaching of fundamental skills to students who are in need of such help.

The Future

We must continue to focus on individual needs and cooperatively search for ways to meet these needs. We have to explore and refine better methods to communicate with parents, continue to search for methods by which children learn best, develop curriculum and materials which allow children to learn naturally and at their own pace, and create an environment where failure becomes an acceptable vehicle for success.

We must continue to determine criteria for evaluating and improving our program. There is also a need to extend our evaluation to the junior and senior high schools. We must be able to establish that our program is essential in the future development of individual children.

Children must be provided with the skills of decision-making. They must be taught to explore alternatives for the solution of problems.

The new teacher is chief diagnostician and learning strategist in the school. Actual implementation of academic programs could be carried out by teacher aides using appropriate media, in conjunction with both professional and community specialists. Rather than a disseminator of knowledge, the new teacher must be one of many resources available to the youngster as he acquires knowledge. Other resources would be the child's classmates, the library, his parents, and the community.

We must continue to make use of educational resources outside of the walls of the school. We must explore ways to involve the community in an educational partnership.

It is the intent of the teachers and the administration of the Paul A. Smith School to have the school become a totally integrated dimension of the community so that school is not just a place that students go "to" and come "from" but one that occupies a real and meaningful part of their everyday lives.

VII

A Flexible Program in a Middle School

Kenneth R. Kimball, Jr.

Flexibility is a key concept at the Alton U. Farnsworth Middle School located in Guilderland, near Albany, New York. A twenty-three module day, with teachers and students determining how time will be used, indicates that this concept really exists in practice. This program has created a truly exciting and dynamic learning environment which strives to prepare young people for full lives in contemporary society.

Not too long ago, teachers, administrators, architects, and members of the community were assembled to plan a new building for Guilderland children. They decided this building must house a quality educational program. As this team visited schools, consulted resource people, and surveyed the literature, they quickly found their dreams could be realized only if they were willing to introduce flexibility into all aspects of the program. This included the flexible use of staff, materials, space, and time.

With this in mind, the committee set about the task of developing an individualized educational program through which each student would perfect those skills necessary to guide his own learning while at the same time exploring numerous areas not formerly open to him. It was further decided that this could best occur in a pleasant atmosphere devoid of the traditional study halls, passes, bells, rigid time schedules, a high degree of competition, locked doors, and the like. During its first two years of operation, the Farnsworth Middle School has taken a giant step in achieving these goals.

This new facility is located on a sixty-four acre suburban tract and provides an outstanding indoor and outdoor environment for learning. The school is composed of three separate buildings, each connected by enclosed corridors. The center structure consists of three academic houses, each having a capacity of 600 students. Each house has students in grades six, seven, and eight. This makes it possible for a student to remain in "his house" for the three years he is in the middle school. He is further assigned to a two, three, or four teacher interdisciplinary team which is responsible for his preparation in language arts, social studies, mathematics, and science. This team also coordinates several other aspects of the child's educational program.

Each house has a house principal, guidance counselor, reading generalist, two foreign language teachers, and a learning workshop teacher. The latter works with students who have problems which limit their learning in a regular classroom situation. A secretary and teaching aide complete the house staff.

Physical education is taught in one of five gymnasiums or on one of several outside play areas. The program stresses lifelong sports but also encourages team participation in both the required classes and intramural program. Electives are offered, as is an adaptive program for selected students.

A large, circular building houses the special area facilities, a cafetorium with three large group rooms, and a spacious learning center. The latter provides space and resources for up to 400 students to learn in a wide variety of interesting situations. Included is a large, horseshoe-shaped room with book and non-book materials. Also located at convenient points are: an audio dial access retrieval system which offers thirty-two different programs, a soft reading area with over one hundred magazines, and microfilm and copy equipment. Separated only by movable bookshelves and cabinets from the open area of the learning center, are individual resource centers for each of the academic subjects and fine arts. The learning center also includes a professional library, a communications center, a television studio and control room, a maintenance shop, audio taping rooms, a planetarium, and a graphic arts production area complete with darkroom and preview room.

Educational Program

One of the first problems faced by the staff at Farnsworth was how to make these valuable resources, both human and material, available to the greatest number of students. Careful analysis of the situation revealed that the answer lay in the flexible use of time. It was further determined that if this time was to be truly flexible, maximum opportunity must be provided for both the students and teachers to determine how a certain student or teacher might spend a given day. Cost alone ruled out a highly sophisticated computerized scheduling program which would respond to the changing needs of more than fifteen hundred students on an hour-to-hour or day-to-day basis. It was soon realized that the greater the opportunity the interdisciplinary teams had to determine how time would be used, the closer the staff would be to reaching its objectives. For this reason, it was decided that a minimum of scheduling would be done by the administration. With this in mind, let's look at a day in the lives of those who are a part of the Farnsworth Middle School.

A Day at Farnsworth

Each day begins with homeroom which lasts for a minimum of fifteen minutes. Students are assigned to a teacher from their interdisciplinary team. During this interval, the teacher completes the customary duties associated with beginning the school day. While this is going on, the students watch a live television news program which is concluded with the opening ceremonies and announcements for the day. This program is produced by students and is transmitted throughout the school.

Following homeroom, the day is divided into twenty-three time blocks called modules. The following schedule illustrates the plan in use during the present school year. It can, of course, be modified to adjust to earlier or later starting times or a longer or shorter day.

8:30	Teachers arrive at school
8:45-9:00	Students arrive at school
9:00-9:15	Homeroom (longer if necessary)
9:15-9:45	Module 1
9:45-3:15	Module 2-23, each module 15 minutes long
3:15	Regular dismissal
3:15-4:00	Activities
4:05	Dismissal for students who stayed for activities
4:15	Teachers depart

Each module, except module one, is fifteen minutes long. The first module purposely includes thirty minutes in order to allow adequate time for extended homeroom activities, television specials, early morning assemblies, and unusual situations such as those created by adverse weather conditions.

The fifteen minute period was selected for each module for a number of reasons. Modules of this duration provide the building blocks necessary to create the wide variety of learning situations expected by the Farnsworth staff. Fifteen minute modules are convenient to work with as they can be easily grouped by both students and teachers. Finally, beginning and ending times of modules are readily visualized on a classroom clock, thus eliminating the need for sounding tones or bells.

Student Schedule

A student's schedule at Farnsworth Middle School will vary from day to day and week to week depending upon a number of factors. One constant, though, is lunch which is scheduled for two modules between 11:00 and 1:00 each day. The greatest variations in time use occur when the student is assigned to his interdisciplinary team. These blocks begin and end at different times for different teams, thus creating a situation where there is no time when all or even a majority of the students are moving about the building at the same time. The schedule below indicates the number of modules reserved for particular activities.

Student Schedule

Activity	*Modules*
Interdisciplinary team (academic areas)	13
Foreign language, remedial program or enrichment activities	2
Special area subjects (either required or elective)	3
Physical education, performing music, learning center, and electives	3
Lunch	2
	23

Interdisciplinary Team

Students are assigned to their interdisciplinary team for thirteen modules each day. There is an effort to place students with wide ranges of ability and interest on each team. An attempt is made to cluster the thirteen modules so that relatively large blocks of time are available. For the most part, interdisciplinary team teachers like the idea of having students for two or three hours of uninterrupted time. The exception, of course, is when this time occurs late in the afternoon.

Each team has one or more teachers who are responsible for language arts, social studies, mathematics, and science. It is then a primary duty of the team working with the guidance counselor and other specialists to set up the learning experiences for each student. This is done in team planning sessions which are held daily for two modules in grade six and on alternate days in grades seven and eight. The house principal, guidance counselor, and various specialists join the team in team meetings.

During these sessions each member is expected to contribute to the long and short term plans of the team. In developing long range plans, they may discuss ways of correlating the various aspects of the curriculum, establish dates for field trips, decide on guest speakers, select dates for large and small group instruction and learning center work. Long range plans would also involve scheduling around assembly programs and testing dates. The important thing is that the teacher or team of teachers who are most affected by the situation are in a position to influence what happens during this time.

In developing short term plans, the team members might decide to have certain students work in the academic resource centers the following day, or perhaps the science teacher might request five modules for lab work. As students are assigned to teams heterogeneously, it is expected that teachers will, from time to time, group students according to achievement, interest, or need. When this occurs, all students on the team must be told where to go at certain times. When a workable plan is developed, the team usually duplicates daily schedules for students, or just announces the various schedules during homeroom. In all cases, teachers have the liberty to set up daily schedules without consultation with the administration.

Foreign Language, Remedial, or Enrichment Time

All sixth grade students and most seventh and eighth grade students take either French or Spanish for two modules each day. In addition, they also spend a minimum of one extra module each week in the language lab. The Farnsworth staff considers two modules daily as very close to the ideal for foreign language instruction in a middle school.

Those students who do not choose to take French or Spanish participate in an alternative program conducted by their teachers which provides remedial help where necessary. This takes place two times each week. It can and often does involve the reading generalist or learning workshop teacher. The remaining three days are scheduled by house principals and guidance counselors who have set up an innovative program of enrichment related to ecology, the world of work, study skills, and various other areas of student interest and need.

Special Area Subjects

Students take art, music, industrial arts, or home economics for at least three modules each day for three-quarters of the year. The special area program is set up on five-week blocks with each student taking at least two five-week blocks of each subject. Home economics and industrial arts are exceptions, with sixth grade boys and girls assigned to five weeks of each subject on a coeducational basis. In seventh and eighth grades only the girls are required to take home economics, while the boys take industrial arts. This schedule leaves students two five-week blocks each year when they can either take special area electives or go to the learning center. As many as two hundred students participate in electives during any five week period. These courses focus on high interest areas and in most cases include sixth, seventh and eighth graders in the same class. Students do not receive marks in electives but do get letters indicating the extent to which they have participated in the course.

Two of the most popular electives offered have been an archeology course with students actually participating in an archeological dig on the site of a one-hundred-year-old school building in the district, and a backpacking course with students meeting every day for five weeks preparatory to a three-day wilderness trip in the Catskill mountains. As an outgrowth of the second program, interest was generated for a two-week, 134-mile trek during the summer. Other electives offered include ceramics, printing, recreational activities, cooking for guys, singing for fun, rocketry, poster fun, creative crafts, artistic metal working, creative holiday decorations, novice amateur radio, social piano, folk guitar, basic drafting, sculpture, environmental art, fashion design, letterpress printing, trampoline, and photography.

The list of special area electives grows each five weeks as teachers determine which courses most interest students. A girl or boy who does not desire to take an elective or does not wish to be in the learning center may choose to work with one of his academic teachers or someone else in the building. He may work in graphics, television, or in the science or language lab. Students do see this as "their" time, which often necessitates adult guidance in selecting suitable activities.

Physical Education, Performing Music, Learning Center, and Electives

Physical education is required of all students on an alternating day basis. Teacher schedules have been set up so that team teaching, coeducational classes, and optional experiences are possible within the regular program. Prior to the opening of the new building, the physical education staff decided to offer a choice of activities during each season of the year. For example, boys are no longer required to play touch football each fall but can now choose from a number of activities including archery, trampoline, cross country, and fly casting. Other interesting activities like advanced gymnastics, snowshoeing, and square dancing under the direction of a professional caller have been added to the program.

On those days when students are not in physical education, they can participate in any one of several performing music groups. With the exception of band and orchestra, it is not possible to practice with more than one group during the regular school day. This has necessitated the formation of several groups which meet during activity time. The learning center is open to all students when they are not in physical education. There are also a number of electives offered on an alternating day basis.

Teacher Schedules

Teacher schedules vary, based on the nature of the subject taught and staff needs during a particular year. Most teachers have students assigned to them for fifteen or sixteen modules each day. Most interdisciplinary team teachers serve for three modules as resource people in the learning center. Here they work with students on regular assignments or enrichment projects. Librarians and aides are also available to serve the several hundred students who use the learning center each day. Special area teachers are assigned to their classrooms which serve as the resource centers for these subjects. They can either work with individual students or offer electives during this time. The remaining five or six modules are used for either individual or team planning and lunch. In addition, teachers are expected to work with students during activity time most days of the week.

Reactions to the Program

Faculty, student, and parent reaction to the flexible program at Farnsworth Middle School has been favorable. All groups were quite understanding when problems arose during our first year of operation. Students have accepted the opportunity to exercise more control over their education with an increased sense of interest and responsibility. Parents report that their youngsters enjoy school. Vandalism is at a new low, even though additional opportunities for trouble are available for the student who desires to seek it. Student use of learning center materials and staff resource people has increased greatly in recent months.

Teachers appear to be working much harder and enjoying it more than they did in our more traditional junior high and elementary schools. On the other hand, although many teachers are effectively individualizing, others are not. Clearer definitions of the basic program and increased supervision and inservice education should make it possible for more teachers to reach this objective.

Interdisciplinary teams also vary in their successes in fully utilizing the modular schedule. They also differ in their progress in becoming truly interdisciplinary. In several cases two or more teachers have team taught for the entire year. There have been total team efforts in anthropology and ecology. Others seem to prefer to work alone. In order to encourage interdisciplinary teaching, each team will conduct at least one interdisciplinary unit each year.

The Future

The staff and students of the Farnsworth Middle School would be the first to suggest that we should continue to move in the direction of more highly individualized instruction. They will also continue to look for ways to increase the student's influence over his own educational program while insuring that the basic goals of education are achieved. Teachers will accelerate their efforts to help students become lifelong learners. It is more than likely that the total community will play a much greater part in reaching this goal.

VIII

A Flexible Program in a High School

Marv Harmon

The Hood River Valley High School Plan is developing out of a concern for improving learning for the youth of our community. The plan began when the people decided to merge two high school plants into one new building.

Teachers were involved in writing educational specifications for the new building; thus existing instructional practices and trends were examined closely. Our goals were to avoid early obsolescence of the building and to create a more humanized environment where increased learning could take place.

Differentiated staffing was selected as a means of realizing a program of continuous progress and individualized learning. The plan has been operational since the fall of 1970. It affects the total student body of approximately 800 and the entire staff of 49 professional Learning Managers, 12 para-professionals, two pre-professionals, a varying number of community associates, and three administrators.

The Hood Plan embodies several flexible procedures to provide better learning. We are convinced that it is impossible to increase learning unless flexibility is built into the program.

The Case of "Randy"

At this point, we introduce "Randy," a hypothetical but typical future learner in our system. As you follow his experiences you will discover the procedures available to insure a flexible, individual, humanized, continuous progress program.

While a ninth grader in one of the local junior high schools, Randy met on several occasions with one or more of our full-time guidance people who explained our system and tried to get to know a little about Randy. He administered a bettery of standardized tests to get more information about Randy's aptitude and abilities. Finally Randy, along with his family, tentatively selected one of the following seventeen clusters: Agriculture, Architecture and Engineering, Bookkeeping, Creative and Communicative Arts, Food Service, General Clerical, General Studies, Health Occupations, Home Economics, Marketing, Industrial Art, Materials Construction, Math and Physical Science, Mechanics and Repairs, Metals, Social Science and Law, and Steno and Secretarial.

Randy must also select a level at which he wants to work within the cluster. There are three: Job Entry, for the learner who will graduate and directly enter the world of work; Technical, designed for the person who will graduate and attend a community college or on-the-job technical training; and College, which is for the college-bound learner.

Randy knows that he may have a change in his cluster and level approved as his abilities and interests become more apparent. He is aware that every class (we call them *mods*) he takes should relate to his cluster and that as soon as he is initially scheduled, he spends two hours a day working directly in his cluster area. Inherent within every cluster are career goals, divided into many areas. Randy's cluster and interests obviously dictate this occupational goal. However, he has many goals other than occupational, including those of citizen, learner, parent, spouse, and community participant.

As he tries to be a positive, productive member of society, all his dreams and aspirations should receive some foundation training. Therefore, with the help of his Guide, Randy will select mods to help him meet his goals in the areas of Effective Living Skills and Basic Learning Skills. For example, all learners take a minimum of four home economics mods. They also take industrial art mods such as Simple Car Repairs and How to Repair Household Items. Business mods designed to create effective living skills, such as typing, income tax, and business machines may be taken on an elective basis.

These are only a few examples of the effective living skills built into each cluster outline. These, as well as the basic learning skills, are not absolute requirements. Each learner is different and every Guide/Learning Manager has the authority and responsibility to guide Randy through the many variations and problems which will arise.

Randy received explanations about the system and made some tentative choices regarding cluster and level. He also selected, if possible, his Guide. If he had no preferences, the guidance department selected a Guide for him. A Guide is a faculty member who is responsible for the academic scheduling and achievement of the approximately 20 students who make up a Guide Group. He also does everything he can to help the students in the Guide Group to become self-actualizing human beings.

Randy is now with a Guide who has a comprehensive cumulative folder which includes test results and anecdotal comments. Before the school year starts, the Guide will schedule an appointment with Randy and his family to discuss the system, answer questions, and establish vital rapport between the school and home. Randy's Guide will make sure that his parents have a Cluster Outline and know how to use it.

The Guide will define a *mod* as a unit of learning which consists of a pre-test, stated performance objectives, and various activities to meet the objectives. When a learner is properly placed, a mod requires approximately 15 hours to complete. The Guide will further explain that grades range from A to C; there are no D's or F's. If a learner does not successfully complete a mod, he simply gets no credit and may take it over. A student may, in the vast majority of cases, complete a mod at his own rate; the 15 hours is truly an approximation. At this point, Randy and his parents usually want to see the scheduling process. Ours is a daily scheduling procedure. The Guide and learner go to the scheduling board and select from a variety of alternatives which exist within the framework of the Cluster Outline.

When Randy reports to a Learning Manager (teacher) to start a required mod, he is given a pre-test. If he scores at a sufficient level, he receives credit for the mod and his Guide is informed. Randy is then rescheduled into a mod which is appropriate to his needs.

The Program Is Assessed

To report programs such as ours and to assure the reader that we are doing the things described is one thing. It is quite another to determine the success of the program. It is easy to praise one's program and have tears, ostensibly of joy, running down cherub-like cheeks without realizing that the tears are created, in fact, by the smoke of the burning building which was set afire by the very learners we are claiming are enraptured with the program. It is a trap into which many educators fall.

In an attempt to avoid this trap and to provide an honest and objective assessment of our success, or lack of it, we are going to summarize the reports of three evaluations which were made during the 1970-71 school year.

The first report was made by Frederick V. Hayen on behalf of the Differentiated Staffing Institute, University of Massachusetts. The second evaluation was conducted by a team from the Oregon Board of Education May 4-6, 1971. The evaluation included a review of the school's self-inventory which is based on Minimum Standards for Public Schools and related educational program guides as adopted by the State Board of Education. The third assessment was made by Ray Talbert and Les Wolfe, from Educational Coordinates.

Without reporting the findings in detail, we list below some of the more pertinent strengths, problems, and conclusions from these assessments.

Program strengths include:

1) Great flexibility—new curriculum can be devised and implemented immediately.
2) Exciting offerings—700 to 800 mods are available; well planned, based upon performance objectives and learning activities.
3) Opportunities for students to explore without serious danger to normal progress—mods are short; lack of success in one does not constitute a catastrophe.
4) Teacher-Guides coupled with a guidance program provide a realistic counseling role for teachers and change professional counseling role to a supporting role for teachers.
5) Student-teacher relationships are good.
6) A dedicated, united school staff is willing to devote many extra hours to improve education for high school youth.
7) Well-developed technical systems handle scheduling, feedback, and record keeping.
8) The superior school plant is designed and constructed to provide maximum flexibility.

Program problems include:

1) The fifteen-hour time factor is limiting flexibility as some teachers seem committed to adhering to it. Learners all begin and end together.
2) Teacher-Guides need to know all the details about the total program; they also need and want more training in counseling techniques.
3) The greatest need is for staff training in: identifying alternatives, resources, and processes in the teaching-learning relationship; management skills; and interpersonal relationship skills.
4) Some students are not responding seriously to the program. Continued attention is needed in the areas of student attitudes, discipline, and school pride.
5) Despite the enormous development in technical and administrative procedures, scheduling problems persist.

A Composite of the Evaluations

It is still too early to determine the success of our program relating to student output. In the spring of 1972 we will be administering the short form of the Iowa Test of Educational Development and will make comparisons with the national norms. Our present sophomore class is our first "pure" group. By the time they are seniors they will have been through the entire program. During the first semester of the last school year our students completed 15,883 mods. During the second semester they finished 20,287 mods. It was during the second semester that our learners began believing that they could really perform at their own rate. At this writing, indications are that a new record will be set.

A survey of our Learning Managers indicates that the quality of work is superior to that received before the program was initiated. Reasons for this improved quality are, in part, the immediate positive response kindled by the mod with its performance objectives and a staff which has actually created a better learning environment.

In the process our staff has overcome many difficulties. One of our administrators was accused of not being aware of problems. So, in an effort to establish rapport, he decided to talk about problems that related to his area at the next faculty meeting. The list was long, and he went over some problems that no other person had perceived. After this discourse, one of the staff said to him, "We have no problems." At this point our administrator felt that someone, either he or the staff member, had gone "crackers." But, after a brief pause, the staff member continued, "We have difficulties we have yet to overcome." That was, and is, the consensus of an outstanding faculty. When you have a group who thinks in such positive terms, everything and anything is possible.

We have encountered the traditional problems of: hesitancy to change, poor communication, independence, "everybody is out of step but me," human identity loss, fighting a new scheduling system, role change, empire building, administrator-teacher gap, paranoia toward community, peers, learners, and self; lack of faith in the program and its leadership, and the like.

We have either beaten or are beating all of these problems. We know that we can handle anything that we encounter as we continue to ride the cutting edge of education.

We strongly believe in an environment for change. By this we mean an honest, open atmosphere, where human beings feel that they can risk ideas and selves without creating or incurring hostility. If staff, students, parents, and community members learn that they are accepting and that they and their views are treated with dignity and truth, many problems dissolve.

We believe that no positive change can take place without positive people. We have provided hours of class, inservice and special time for our staff to learn techniques of communication and interpersonal relations. Few people like change, but the rewards have been great.

We still have people who don't believe in the program, and we probably always will. These people are important because they keep us from growing stagnant and they often have good ideas that we can incorporate. Whenever a person or a group does express discontent, we meet with them and listen. Then we try to give honest responses.

Our doors are always open to members of our community, but we still have major problems with communication. People respond emotionally to a rumor, and it becomes difficult to find the catalyst that started it all. To help overcome this difficulty each Guide *must* communicate a minimum of six times with the parents of his guidees.

We have been asked to ". . . indicate exactly how the program *has been* and *is* being financed." That is always a problem. Briefly, our program has been financed by an unusually supportive school board as well as by the Oregon Compact, Region VII of the Oregon Council for Curriculum Improvement, The Oregon State Board of Education, EPDA, Title III, and various other federal and state grants. One other resource with countless dollars that is often overlooked is the substantial amount of uncounted time poured into the program by a selfless, dedicated staff.

It is, partly, this dedication of the staff which will insure that the program will continue. The program will continue and expand, also, because the most important people in it, the learners, do not want to "go back" to a traditional program. We have diffused the leadership. Consequently, the program will not die when the initial change agents leave because everyone is a change agent. All are involved somewhere on the leadership continuum.

The program will expand as we become more flexible. The fairly restrictive cluster outlines currently in effect will soon be redesigned so that concepts are stated in performance terms. Then each mod will be related to the concept to be learned from it. Obviously, each concept may have an infinite number of mods related to it. The learner will complete whatever number of mods are necessary in order to demonstrate that he has attained the performance objectives stated in the concept at that level which is essential to his career goals. This new structure will create a highly flexible elective high school program. It will be possible for all learning to be individually designed for each student.

The program will also expand as more and more staff are willing to take high risks for high gains. Our young people are finding that learning can be fun. More of our dropouts are coming back because they don't face a wall of D's and F's. The program enhances our efforts to meet the needs of all of our learners, not only the upper third who go to college. Finally, we believe this program will continue and expand because it encourages the development of trust among human beings. Visitors tell us they can feel this trust in the school atmosphere.

IX

The Ninety Six Story

Catherine Johnson

Ninety Six High School is located in a rural-textile community in the Piedmont area of South Carolina. The population of this independent school district is approximately 5,000 with about 1,400 school age children attending Ninety Six Elementary (500), Ninety Six Middle (460), and Ninety Six High (380-400). The High School staff includes a principal, curriculum coordinator, assistant to the superintendent, counselor, librarian, twenty-four classroom teachers, two aides, one secretary, and three clerk-typists. The tax base is sufficiently broad enough to provide a $540 expenditure per pupil each year. The local supplement to teacher salaries ranks first in the state.

The innovative program of Ninety Six High School is a combination of multi-level grouping and individualized progress curriculum through teacher-prepared Learning Activity Packages. Planning for the program began in September, 1968. During the 1969-70 school year, administrators and teachers visited schools which were using multi-level grouping and individual learning units.

Final plans were made for the Ninety Six program to begin in September, 1970. Two three-week workshops were held during July, 1970 and 1971, during which a Ninety Six Format for the Learning Activity Package (LAP) was developed, and teachers wrote LAPs in their subject area for use during the 1970-71 and 1971-72 school years.

Funds to help with implementing the program have been provided by the South Carolina Desegregation Committee and Title III ESEA.

The goals of the program are to:

1) Develop a multi-level curriculum which will provide for the diversity of achievement among students.

2) Develop an organized system of individual progress which will embrace a diversity of learning rates.
3) Raise the mean achievement level of all students.
4) Develop a more positive attitude toward learning.

Grouping Procedures

Flexibility in the program is achieved in both the grouping and instructional procedures. In the first year (9th grade) the students were grouped into four levels based upon their performance on a standard achievement test. Those scoring below the twentieth percentile were placed in Level 1, those with scores falling from the 21st through the 39th percentile in Level 2, those with scores from the 40th through the 64th percentile in Level 3, and those with scores at the 65th percentile or above in Level 4. During the second year of the program, grouping was primarily by student choice. Individual guidance was provided by the counselor and teachers, after which students were assigned to the level of their choice.

Level 1 may be described as appropriate for students who need special assistance, who plan to enroll in vocational courses, and who score at stanines 1 or 2 on achievement tests. Level 2 includes students who need help on basic skills, who plan to enroll in vocational or business courses and who score at stanines 2 or 3 on achievement tests. Level 3 meets the needs of average students who may be interested in college, technical school, or business training, who will do the average amount of studying, and who score at stanines 4, 5, or 6 on achievement tests. Level 4 is designed for well-prepared students who plan further education after high school, who have better than average grades, who will do more than the minimum required work, and who score at stanines 7, 8, or 9 on achievement tests.

During both the first and second years, students have been moved from one level to another in both directions. This is done in consultation with teachers, students, and parents. Reasons for change of level include failure to succeed at a high level, frustration because of difficulty of work, and lack of challenge because of easy work at a low level.

Students are scheduled at different levels according to their capabilities in different subjects. For example, a student who is very capable in English and social studies but weak in math would be scheduled at a high level in English and social studies and a lower level in mathematics. In general, home economics, art, industrial arts (shop), music, and physical education classes are heterogeneous and are not classified according to level.

Learning Activity Packages

Flexibility is an inherent characteristic of the instructional program which consists of highly structured, teacher-written

Learning Activity Packages. A comprehensive scope and sequence plan has been written by classroom teachers for each discipline. Each item in the scope and sequence framework is a topic which has been (or will be) developed into a LAP. LAPs are written for each of the four levels. Each LAP follows the format shown in Figure 1.

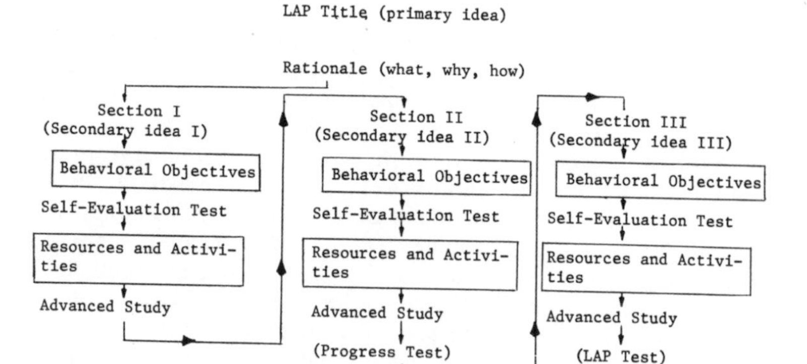

Fig. 1. LAP Format - Ninety Six High School

Each LAP may have as many or as few sections as are necessary to cover the primary idea. Each section may have as many or as few behavioral objectives as are necessary to cover the secondary idea.

The two most important parts of each LAP are the Behavioral Objectives and the Resources and Activities. Through these, any degree of flexibility desired by both teacher and learner may be achieved. The teacher is free to prescribe for each individual, and, within the teacher's prescription, the learner is free to choose the resources and activities which he prefers.

The statement of Behavioral Objectives follows that described by Robert Mager in his book *Preparing Instructional Objectives* (1) and includes all levels of objectives as described by Bloom, *et al.* in *Taxonomy of Educational Objectives: Cognitive Domain.* (2) Included in the Behavioral Objectives is a statement of how the student will be evaluated. Some of the methods of evaluation are teacher conference, small and large group discussion, oral and written reports, essays, themes, papers of varying lengths and, or course, written objective and essay tests.

The Resource and Activities part of the LAP lists all resources to which the student may go to learn what he needs to know to reach the behavioral objectives. These resources include the basic textbook and several supplementary texts, reference books, audio tapes, filmstrips, and films. All activities which will aid him in his learning are given. Any required resources and activities are checked, and any additional ones which the teacher may prescribe are checked for individual students.

Evaluation procedures are clearly stated throughout the LAP. Each behavioral objective contains a statement such as, "After completing your prescribed course of study, you will be able to state four causes of the American Civil War. You will demonstrate this ability in small group discussion and on the progress test." The small group discussion will be formed by students or teachers at a time agreed upon by both. The student asks for permission to take the written progress test whenever he has completed the required and prescribed activities and has indicated a readiness through successful mastery of the items in the self-evaluation test which is included in the LAP.

Advanced Study Activities are included for those students who want to go beyond the minimum required work. These activities are related to concepts covered in the behavioral objectives and involve study in depth, creative work, and other items of interest to some students which could not be included in the required work because of time or difficulty. Some teachers may require completion of one or more advanced study activities for certain students or for a specific quality grade.

Because the nature of the program itself introduced a totally different method of teaching and learning which we expected would be difficult for parents and students to accept, it was decided not to make any major changes in the way grades or progress was reported to parents. A traditional letter grade (A, B, C, D, F) system has been used for many years with report cards issued each six weeks. This system has been used this year on a new tear-away type of report which was designed to reflect the new curriculum and its requirements.

The Progress Report includes: a letter grade for quantity which is determined by the amount of work the student has completed during the report period (regardless of quality); a letter grade for the quality of work completed during the report period (regardless of quantity), and a letter grade for any LAP test taken during the report period. The Progress Report also shows the LAP range for that particular subject and the LAP on which the student is working at the time. These last two items provide parents with a gauge to the student's rate of working and indicate whether completion of the course is likely within the current school year.

Since one of the unstated aims of the program is to eliminate failure, a student does not progress to more difficult material until he has succeeded on the easier material. If he fails at the first trial, he recycles until he succeeds. Many recyclings may indicate the student is working at too high a level, wasting time, or trying to get by without learning the material. Recycling is time consuming and will impede progress on the horizontal plane which may require extra time on the course. Recycling is also indicated on the Progress Report.

Administrative Problems

Two important administrative decisions with respect to this innovative program were based upon a careful reassessment of the staff resources (teachers, administrators, clerical help) and of the use of existing space within the building. Since the staffing item was considered to be most important, the decision was made to expend funds on additional teachers, typists, and an administrator, and to use our existing space without additional expenditures.

Through the help of Title III, ESEA, and ESAP, the classroom teacher staff was increased so that no teacher who is writing LAPs has more than four classes per day. This gives the teacher two full class periods each day for writing. We have estimated that about thirty to thirty-five teacher hours go into the writing of each LAP. This, of course, is in addition to the usual grading of papers, preparation, setting up labs, etc., which continue to be part of a teacher's day. Sufficient funds have also been available to periodically hire a substitute teacher to relieve a teacher for two full days to write LAPs at school.

At the present time, the writing is proceeding on schedule; teachers have the succeeding LAPs ready when the students are ready. Since only revisions are anticipated for years following the current one, the teacher-time problem is expected to diminish each year. Title III funds will expire in May, 1974, and a return to a normal teacher load of five classes is anticipated at that time.

After the teachers have written the LAPs, they must be printed in sufficient quantities to provide one copy for each student who will use them, and to meet the requirements of the Title III project of supplying copies for each school district in South Carolina and for state evaluation. A clerical staff of three typists and offset machine operators is employed full time to fill this requirement. They are paid from ESEA and ESAP funds. This staff will probably be reduced to two persons upon the expiration of federal funds.

A full-time Project Coordinator is also paid from ESEA funds. The Coordinator is the former principal of the school who helped develop the program as it is today. He is responsible for coordinating all writing and use of LAPs in the classrooms, for reviewing all LAPs for content and format, for dissemination, and for all record keeping connected with expenditures from the federal programs. It is expected that a Coordinator will be needed after federal funds expire, and this cost will be assumed by the school district.

The program has increased the work load of the guidance counselor who has assisted in developing and coordinating the program. The nature of the students' learning environment has tripled the number of individual conferences concerning choice and levels of courses and learning difficulties.

Two teacher aides have been employed who assist in the Resource Center, the Test Center, or wherever needed. The library aide is also essential to the operation of the program.

Since no additional space was available, the existing space had to be used to better advantage. An excellent, traditional library which served as a place for books and quiet reading was already available. It was converted into a modern Resource Center with carrels for individual use of cassette players and filmstrip viewers, tables for group listening and viewing, and storage for the increased number and kind of multi media and multi-level reading materials. This was done with the addition of only one existing storage room to the library area.

The Resource Center is a beehive of activity during all periods of the school day. Purposeful use of the center has increased by 50 percent over other years, and it is expected that additional space will be required when the total curriculum is developed into LAPs.

Because the structure of the LAP allows students to reach the Progress and LAP test point at different times, entire class test administration is inappropriate. This has necessitated establishing a Test Center where students write Progress and LAP tests for all courses in the curriculum which are taught with LAPs. The Test Center is open each class period and is staffed by a classroom teacher or aide. Students come to the Center from the subject teacher who indicates on a written pass the subject, section number, and form of the test which the student is to write. The student writes the test in the Center using whatever aids the test allows. The tests are returned by the Test Center staff to the subject teacher for grading.

All tests for subjects taught on LAPs are kept in the locked storage room in the Test Center. As each LAP is written, three forms of all tests prescribed by the LAP are also written, printed, and placed on file in the Center. The tests must adhere to the behavioral objectives prescribed in the LAP.

Classroom space continues to be limited to nonflexible, thirty to forty student capacity, traditional classrooms. The need is being felt for space for small group work apart from the larger group and for space for larger group sessions. Additional space must come from local funds. These items are not top priority in the local budget at this time.

Evaluation of the Program

At this time the success of the program can be stated in terms of process only. The Title III ESEA timetable is being met; that is, we estimate about 40 percent of the curriculum (Levels 3 and 4 in all grades) is being taught using LAPs. Teachers are writing to keep ahead of students. The timetable calls for 70 percent of the curriculum to be written into LAPs by September, 1972, and 100 percent by September, 1973. It is anticipated that we will be able to adhere to this timetable.

Success in terms of student output cannot be evaluated at this time. A standardized achievement test administered to 9th grade students in March, 1971, in our school and in a neighboring traditional school is one basis for evaluation. The same two groups of students will be tested each spring with the final evaluation of the results to come in the spring of 1974. An instrument measuring attitudes toward school will be administered periodically to students in Ninety Six High School through the spring of 1974. A follow-up of the 1974 graduates will be made to determine how many have entered post high school educational institutions and how many are enrolled in advanced college courses.

Problems in Implementation

The greatest problem encountered in implementing the program has been in helping the students to assume their responsibility in their new role of learner. Almost every student was introduced to the LAP during the 1970-71 school year, instructed in its use, and supposedly prepared for 100 percent exposure during the 1971-72 school year. Students were made aware of the LAP range of each course and of the estimated timetable for completion.

The concept of total responsibility for working each day and of pacing themselves was an unfamiliar and uncomfortable one for students. "Freedom of choice" led many to choose to do nothing. Many teacher, counselor, and principal hours have been spent in parent conferences in an effort to solve this problem. Community meetings were held in the spring of 1971 and in the fall of 1971 in an effort to avoid these situations, but attendance was slight. More meetings are being scheduled in the near future to try to prevent further problems.

The scope and sequence for each course was established by classroom teachers using traditional textbooks and personal preferences as guides. Teacher intuition has influenced the amount of material included in each LAP. At this point, a reevaluation of the number of LAPs required for each course and the amount of work in each LAP seems inevitable. It appears that successful completion of this curriculum as it is being written may require the average student more than nine months. Since a longer school year is impractical, the material may need to be shortened.

The greatest problem encountered with teachers has been in helping them to develop sufficient self-confidence to write LAPs without assistance. This probably stems from undue reliance on textbooks in previous years and in their narrow range of experience with supplementary resource materials within their subject fields. The "best" teachers in a traditional system are the "best" LAP writers in this system because they have a broader background from which to draw and have a variety of methods in their already good repertoire.

It appears that some teachers with many years of experience may have difficulty in adjusting to this program. The teachers who seem to have less difficulty adapting are those with sufficient experience to feel confident in the subject matter but not enough to have firmly established more rigid classroom techniques.

Teachers as well as students have experienced difficulties in learning to use the LAP. The teacher problems in the use of the LAP in the classroom have centered around trying to help each student individually and ignoring the continued usefulness of group activity. The same question is answered thirty times for thirty individual students when it could have been handled more efficiently for the entire group. Many teachers have allowed students to pace themselves entirely and have not adequately monitored the work until the student was considerably behind. This may indicate a need for more supervision of teachers.

There have been no problems with financing. ESEA has provided funds for staff and materials for printing. The school district has provided all additional funds for books and equipment for the instructional programs. It is anticipated that the school district will be able to handle the necessary financing when the federal funds expire.

Future Plans

The administration, faculty and Board of Trustees of Ninety Six High School are committed to the full implementation of this program in the school. Unless serious unforseen difficulties arise, it will be continued after the expiration of federal funds. The groundwork is being laid to implement a similar program in the Middle School which feeds the High School.

Notes

(1) Robert F. Mager, *Preparing Instructional Objectives* (Palo Alto, Cal.: Fearon Publishers, 1962.)

(2) Benjamin S. Bloom, ed., *Taxonomy of Educational Objectives, The Classification of Educational Goals, Handbook I: Cognitive Domain* (New York: David McKay Company, Inc., 1956).

X

Critique

Willard J. Congreve
and George J. Rinehart

Two practitioners have taken time from their normal routines to identify schools which seem to be doing things a bit differently. Even though we have done little more than get a picture of the efforts of some impatient and creative educators, have we learned anything to suggest where schools might be heading in the future? We think we have.

What seems to be taking place? While the initial action taken by a school to increase flexibility might be the adoption of a single procedure, once underway the school often finds itself adding additional procedures in a short time. We suspect that adoption of such procedures is not in response to a fundamental change in educators' views about their responsibilities to children. Rather, it appears that they have discovered that the monolithic lessons taught to age-grade groups in "egg-crate" school buildings are not reaching children and are not sacrosanct.

At this point in time, schools are in the "doing something" stage. They have not settled down to a "new program." At one point in our study we thought we might arrive at a description of the model flexible school of the future. We find we are not able to do so on the basis of our data. But the multi-dimensional descriptions presented herein suggest a number of ways to achieve flexibility in school programs.

What forces are causing these things to happen? The complex human and physical resources interacting in this process defy simplistic explanations. Leadership seems essential in overcoming inertia. This leadership usually comes from top administrators, at least from the principal. But once momentum is established and the atmosphere conducive to trying out ideas is created, procedures are often planned and implemented by teachers and other staff.

In most instances, the process has not been one of abandoning everything and creating a new learning situation from scratch. Although some new schools have built these procedures into their programs from the outset, in most it has been a somewhat gradual adoption of one procedure, which then leads to another and another. Once the administration and school board have committed themselves to providing several learning options, the possibilities seem unlimited.

Several other forces have encouraged change. Federal funds have been extremely helpful, especially those which have been available through ESEA Title III. New building designs, while not essential to the adoption of many procedures, have stimulated schools to refashion programs. The Educational Facilities Laboratory (477 Madison Avenue, New York, N. Y., 10022) has encouraged new school designs since 1957 and has provided support for schoolmen and board members desiring to learn about them. Other agencies and programs have also been extremely instrumental in influencing the direction of change.

Competition among schools and districts has also encouraged change. Although there is little question that adopting procedures to meet the learning needs of individual children requires considerable additional effort and commitment from teachers, they evidently feel that this additional expenditure of time and energy is worth it.

What makes change last? What perpetuates the desire to continue to move forward? Part of the answer to this question comes from the nature of man. Despite evidence which describes man as a resister of change, deep within him is a psychological need to identify and to solve problems. But other factors also operate. Success encourages more daring adventures. In almost no time a successful student-choice schedule seems like old hat, and the designers are busy figuring out other options to adopt. Success in one school is usually sufficient to encourage others to try similar programs. Despite the fact that only a minority of American schools have adopted procedures to achieve flexibility, the number is growing constantly. Hardly a new school facility has been constructed in the past decade which does not provide resource centers, flexible space, and various sized instructional areas, all conducive to these procedures.

How are these procedures being accepted? We began our work on this book with several hunches about persons or groups who are strongly opposed to these procedures. We finish our endeavor with most of these hunches tempered considerably. Schools which have implemented a large number of procedures find themselves out in front of their communities. This can be uncomfortable. Nevertheless, community response has been quite good. But school people need to work doubly hard to nourish such support.

Although community resistance is rather mild, it seems to be coming from a minority of people who have the strength of voice to be heard. They are raising questions which deserve the attention of educators:

1) Many programs have been described with words such as: "The school has become a natural and a pleasant place. The concept of failure has been removed." Are these ideas the adult can tolerate? Should they tolerate them? Should the atmosphere and demands be different for children at differing levels of their development?
2) Most reported results of programs indicate no increase in achievement in those aspects of learning which adults have used to evaluate schools in the past. Should society accept the additional goals and outcomes of these procedures as valuable in light of no improvement in basic skills?

Teacher acceptance has been outstanding, especially when they have been given time and assistance to upgrade their knowledge, redesign their teaching strategies, and obtain new materials. The excellent, creative teacher has seen this movement toward flexibility as a means of creating a new era of educational excitement. Little resistance has come from teacher organizations or unions.

The primary objective of the new procedures is to help individual children achieve success. If educators can demonstrate progress toward this goal, it is doubtful that the procedures will be seriously challenged in democratic America.

Nevertheless, in the face of even the slightest adversity, the broader the commitment in the school district, the greater the chances for the survival of new practices. District-wide staff, board, and superintendent commitment will go a long way to insure success and perpetuation. Community involvement in planning and designing the procedures is also an excellent way to broaden support. It appears to us from our data that there may be occasional instances of retreating, regrouping of forces, and redesigning of programs, but we believe that this will be temporary.

What other problems confront the efforts to achieve flexibility? Are they really serious? New programs often cost money. Schools are facing a crisis in financing, which may slow down efforts to become more flexible. However, with the shifting of priorities, schools may be able to survive the temporary money squeeze. Some procedures, it should be noted, can actually save money.

Teacher education institutions must become more vigorous in preparing teachers to function in flexible, option-filled programs. Our data indicate that most beginning teachers emerge from their period of training unprepared to function effectively in this kind of educational milieu. This, too, should become less of a problem as the surplus of teachers increases. As school districts demand teachers who have these new skills, universities have to change their training programs accordingly. It is unfortunate that some teacher education institutions view their role primarily as a trainer of persons to fill existing positions rather than as leaders of thought in education and preparers of scholar-teachers capable of giving leadership in the processes of education.

Leadership in local districts is becoming less of a problem. The quality and number of workshops, refresher courses, and institutes available to administrators and board members is rapidly creating a core of leaders prepared to influence constructive change in schools.

It appears to us that one of the greatest problems confronting many educators who are attempting to develop programs to provide for the learning needs of individual children is the fuzzy definition which currently exists for "individualized instruction." We should like to point out a few of the partial understandings which are compounding the difficulty.

As we see it, providing for the learning needs of individual children means giving each child just what he needs to learn most effectively and efficiently. This definition is the ideal, a goal toward which educators should strive. However, as long as schools are organized for group instruction and are limited in the number of persons and resources available, they can expect to fall short of this goal.

But we believe that even within these limitations, considerable progress can be made in the direction of providing for the learning needs of individual children. Let us take a look at the misconceptions.

Many people thinking about individualized instruction believe that:

1) It involves students accepting responsibility for their own learning and when they do not accept this responsibility, the program is not working.

   Not so. Independence in learning is different from individualized instruction. Both the independent and the dependent learner progress under individualized instruction. Each is given the proper amount of guidance and direction needed to cause him to learn. The child who needs to be told exactly what to do, when, and how, will be told in an individualized instruction setting. An additional goal might be to make the dependent learner independent, self-directing and responsible. If that is the case, the kinds of guidance and direction given him will be tailored to help him learn how to reach this additional goal.

2) All children must be doing something differently.

   Not true. If what is to be learned is appropriate for ten, twenty, or 100 children at one time, there is no reason why they cannot learn it as a group. As long as they all need it and are ready for the same level learning experience, the teacher is providing for their individual learning needs even though all are doing it together.

3) The teacher must personally explain the same thing thirty different times.

Not true. Readiness is a flexible concept. Johnny may be ready right now, but this could be delayed a few moments or a day or so until three or four others were also ready, and the explanation could be made to more students. Although there is what Havighurst has called the "teachable moment," that moment is not a specific second in a child's life, but rather is a fairly lengthy time span when motivation and readiness are high.

4) Children should always be working by themselves.

   Not true. Nothing can be more boring than to have to work alone all the time. Excellent learning takes place under pleasant conditions for people who enjoy working together. More and more adults are doing this all the time.

5) Packets and contracts are essential to providing for the learning needs of individual children.

   Not true. They can be helpful, but they can also be an interference. The important thing is the cooperative diagnosis involving student and teacher, the identification of what should be learned next, and the determining of the materials, equipment and processes needed for learning. It is the availability of a variety of materials and techniques which is important.

We could go on. The key to the issue is our definition—doing the best possible job of giving each child what he needs at a particular time to cause his learning to go forward. To be sure, the more resources available, the more options at the teacher's command, and the greater the understanding about learning, the closer one can come to reaching this goal. But it is a goal, not a procedure. The teacher who is committed to providing for the learning needs of individual children will use any number of procedures along the continuum from totally teacher-directed to totally student-directed learning activities.

All in all, if we can agree that providing for the learning needs of individual children is important, and that to do so, flexibility or multiple learning options are required, then we must conclude that the public schools of America are definitely on a positive course for improvement. Some critics notwithstanding, in our view, American schools are healthy and becoming healthier by the moment.

Appendix A
Categories of Procedures to Achieve Flexibility in Schools

The categories of procedures described below evolved from our inquiry. In inviting school people to tell us about their programs, we provided each with a Select-O-Sheet questionnaire which listed nine different procedures generated from our personal experience as educators and from a routine study of the literature. In addition, we invited our respondents to describe procedures which did not fit the categories we provided. The questionnaire responses supplied the major data for building the categories.

Initially, we became entangled in terminology. We began by using the word *innovation.* We soon discovered that we could not distinguish among practices which were innovative and those which were not. Many procedures currently considered innovative are as old as education itself (e.g., multi-age or family grouping began in the one-room rural school house). Therefore, we abandoned *innovation* and substituted *procedure.*

As the categories of procedures were being generated and definitions established, they were critiqued by other experts knowledgeable in the field. Critics included: Mrs. Joan Beers, Office of Educational Research and Statistics, Department of Public Instruction, Commonwealth of Pennsylvania; Dr. Paul B. Campbell, Educational Testing Service, Princeton, New Jersey; Dr. Reginald A. Corder, Professional Associate, Advisory Services, Western Office, Educational Testing Service, Berkeley, California; Dr. Marcus A. Foster, Superintendent of Schools, Oakland, California; and Dr. James Scammon, Administrator of Planning and Research, Kenosha Unified Schools, Kenosha, Wisconsin.

We turn now to the categories:

Instructional Plans to Meet Individual Learning Needs

For the most part, procedures to achieve flexibility have the basic purpose of creating instructional plans to meet individual learning needs or to achieve individualized instruction. In general, these procedures make it possible to:

1) Have students in the same grade or group work on different materials or at different levels in the same materials;
2) Have groups include children of different age or grade levels, especially in elementary schools;
3) Eliminate grade designations;
4) Have sub-group instruction directed toward the particular learning needs of each sub-group in a class;
5) Diagnose the level of learning of each child and provide regular feedback to check progress;
6) Have children learn through the use of different media—audio, visual, tactile, etc.;
7) Have children participate in planning and/or directing some aspects of their learning (What? How? When? or Where?)

More specific procedures to attain these ends are included in the categories which follow.

Diagnostically Guided Prescribed Learning

Diagnostically guided prescribed learning is a systematic plan guided by well-defined objectives. It involves diagnosis to determine the point at which instruction is to begin, evaluation of diagnostic data, identification of learning needs, planning of learning tasks, continuous monitoring of progress and rediagnosis leading to recycling of the process. The learner is not bound to tasks set for other children. Neither is he expected to maintain a pace set by others.

Independent Learning or Contract Learning

The student selects topics, problems, or questions to investigate. His selection may be made in cooperation with the teacher or independently. In the latter case it is understood that whatever the student selects will have the approval of the teacher. Similarly, a plan of investigation is established either in cooperation with the teacher or independently. Upon completion of the work, the student is credited for its completion. He may receive a critique from which he can get a sense of recognition for his accomplishment.

Team Planning and Teaching

Team planning and teaching involves two or more teachers working together with a common group of children, using planning time to divide up responsibilities, and agreeing upon roles to carry out the instructional program. The roles may remain constant over a period of time or may change according to an agreed upon schedule.

Differentiated Staffing

In a differentiated staffing arrangement, roles and responsibilities are defined for such personnel as Master or Head Teacher, Teacher, Scheduler, Paraprofessional, Volunteer, Student Teacher, Cadet Teacher, Peer Tutor, Secretary. Among the functions to be performed are these: diagnostician and organizer of learning activities; prescriber and supervisor of learning activities; preparer of materials; supervisor of material distribution; data analyzer or evaluator, who feeds information back to the diagnostician; supervisor of non-teaching activities.

Scheduling

The purpose of scheduling is to provide differential time blocks for various programs of study. Options may be provided for places where students can go during the school day, for students to select staff and other resources related to their programs of study, for teachers to carry on planning activities, for student-teacher planning. Scheduling may also be concerned with times for learning outside the regular school hours—nights, summers, weekends, the year-round school.

The Open Classroom

The concept of the open classroom implies room for more than one conventional class in a single facility. There are interest centers or perhaps an adjoining instructional materials center. More than one activity takes place simultaneously. Students have freedom to move from one activity or center to another. Two or more teachers are working in the area. Space is provided to allow maximum flexibility in the utilization of the facilities.

The Open Study Hall

More than one place is provided where students may go to study. The student is free to choose among the places available, such as the library, a resource center, a learning center, etc. He may move from one study area to another at any time or at times specified for the purpose.

The Open Campus

In a fully open campus students are required to be at designated places only when a definite appointment has been established (a regularly scheduled class, a small group meeting, or individual instruction). At other times students are free to come and go as they please, except to areas designated as "off limits."

In a partially open campus certain limitations may be set, such as a uniform reporting time for all students, a stipulation as to the number of study hall or library periods a student must attend prior to exercising open campus privileges, qualifications which must be met before the privilege of open campus may be granted (minimum grade average, parent permission, minimum grade level, etc.)

Educational Technology

Technology can provide equipment to be used by individual learners or small groups of learners and can provide for differences in learning preferences among students. With appropriate software, entire programs can be developed around technology, providing materials at different levels of difficulty. Technology can speed up information processing for the purpose of diagnosis, monitoring, feedback.

Unique Curricula

Flexibility may be provided through the development of curriculum programs which depart from conventional offerings. Examples are programs in black studies; programs for particular groups of students, such as dropouts, potential dropouts, preschoolers; programs for career education; programs taking advantage of community resources; programs to develop special talents of all kinds; programs in the creative arts.

Mini-Courses

Mini-courses are most commonly found in junior and senior high schools. They require less time than conventional course—a few hours, a few days, or a few weeks. They focus on more limited areas of a subject than the conventional Carnegie unit course, providing opportunity for in-depth study. Students can select from a number of mini-courses so as to follow personal interests and aptitudes or to explore new fields. Mini-courses could be scheduled during an interim between semesters as well as during the regular school year.

Use of Resources Not Regularly Provided by Schools

Courses, mini-courses, or particular units may be taught by persons other than regular school personnel, either in the school or outside the school. Students are permitted to take college courses on nearby campuses, receiving both college and high school credit for their work. High school courses may be taken for credit toward graduation on an optional basis, either during the day or in evening classes. In cooperative education programs students may work part time and simultaneously receive high school credit.

Appendix B

Schools and School Districts Participating in the Survey

The following schools or school districts which participated in the survey have been grouped according to the major thrust of the programs underway as determined from their reports to the editors of this volume. Usually this thrust includes more than one of the procedures described in Appendix A.

Community Involvement

West Side High School, 9th and Gerry Streets, Gary, Indiana 46406. Dr. David W. Hennage.
Baltimore City Public Schools, 3 East 25th St., Baltimore, Maryland 21218. Dr. Vernon Vevrirada.
Flint Community Schools, 923 E. Kearsley Street, Flint, Michigan 48502. Mr. David S. Beavers.
Tupelo Public Schools, Tupelo, Mississippi. Dr. C. E. Holladay.
Herricks Public Schools, Shelter Rock Road, New Hyde Park, New York 11040.
Parkway High School, Philadelphia, Pennsylvania. Mr. Leonard B. Finkelstein.

Comprehensive Approach

Tucson Public School, District #1, Project CREATES, Tucson, Arizona 85717. Mr. Ronald L. DeWitt.
Lynch Drive Elementary School, North Little Rock, Arkansas. Mr. George Miller.
Oberon Junior High School, 7300 Quail Street, Arvada, Colorado 80002. Mr. Stewart Frew.
Cherry Creek Public Schools, 4700 S. Yosemite St., Englewood, Colorado 80110. Dr. Edward Pino.
Walnut Hills Elementary School, Cherry Creek Schools #5, Englewood, Colorado. Dr. Dave Mathias.
Grand Junction Public Schools, 2115 Grand Avenue, Grand Junction, Colorado 81501. Mr. Tedd Brumbaugh.
Meeker Public Schools, P. O. Box 159, Meeker, Colorado 81641. Mr. Robert E. King.
North Haven High School, North Haven, Connecticut. Dr. Del Rolundo.
Dickinson High School, Stanton School District, 1800 Limestone Road, Stanton, Wilmington, Delaware 19804. Mr. William P. Keim.

Cocoanut Creek Elementary Schools, Broward County Schools, Fort Lauderdale, Florida 33310. Mrs. Williamson.
Leo High School, 14600 Amstutz Road, Grabill, Indiana 46741. Mr. Loren Jones.
Lebanon Community School Corporation, 404 N. Meridian Street, Lebanon, Indiana 46052. Mr. Gordon Ruff.
Newton Community School District, 807 South 6th Avenue West, Newton, Iowa 50208. Willard J. Congreve.
Louisville Public Schools, 506 West Hill Street, Louisville, Kentucky 40208. Dr. Norman Walker.
East Baton Rouge Parish School Board, P. O. Box 2950, Baton Rouge, Louisiana 70821. Mr. Robert J. Aertker.
St. Bernard Parish School, Chalmette, Louisiana 70043. Mrs. Imogene Renshaw and Mr. Buford Jones.
Bancroft Elementary School, Andover, Massachusetts 01810. Mr. Earl E. Simon.
Meadowbrook Junior High School, Newton, Massachusetts.
Oak Grove Junior High School, 1300 W. 106th St., Bloomington, Minnesota 55431. Mr. Fred Atkinson.
Wilson Campus School, School of Education, Mankato State College, Mankato, Minnesota 56001. Dr. Donald Glines.
North Junior High School, Great Falls School District, Great Falls, Montana 59403. Dr. Russell S. Carlson.
Ruby S. Thomas Elementary School, Las Vegas, Nevada. Mr. William Wallin.
Englewood Public Schools, 51 Englewood Avenue, Englewood, New Jersey 07631. Mr. Peter J. Dugan.
Albuquerque Public Schools, Box 1927, Albuquerque, New Mexico 87100. Mr. Michael White.
Cassadaga Valley Central School, Sinclairville, New York 14782. Mr. Frederick L. Wilson.
Mariemont City School District, 3810 Pocahontas, Cincinnati, Ohio 45227. Mr. Robert W. Crabbs.
John Adams High School, Portland Unified District, Portland, Oregon. Mr. Robert Schwartz.
Chesapeake Demonstration School, Chesapeake Public Schools, Chesapeake, Virginia. Mr. Joseph A. Peele and Mr. Thomas A. Felton, Jr.
Robinwood Elementary School, 10700 West Church Street, Franklin, Wisconsin 53132. Mr. R. J. Ziegler.
Van Buren Elementary School, 315 South Jackson Street, Janesville, Wisconsin 53545. Mrs. Ethel Arentsen.

Continuous Progress, Nongradedness, Multi-Age Grouping

Conway High School, Conway, Arkansas. Mr. James Clark.
Granada Community School and Demonstration Center, Reed Union School District, 50 El Camino, Corte Madera, California 94925. Mr. Edward Mosconi.
Rincon School, Livermore School District, 1251 Rincon Avenue, Livermore, California 94550. Mr. Walter Capri.
Woodlake Union High School, 400 West Whitney Avenue, Woodlake, California 93286. Mr. Ellsworth Loverin.
Avon Public Schools, Avon, Connecticut. Dr. Hubert Pandiscio.
Milford School, 906 Lakeview Avenue, Milford, Delaware 19963. Mr. James Kerr.
Burris Laboratory School, Ball State University, Muncie, Indiana 47306. Dr. Kenneth Foster.
Urbandale Public Schools, 7101 Airline Avenue, Urbandale, Iowa 50322. Dr. L. Kehn.
Apollo Elementary School, Bossier Parish School Board, P. O. Box 218, Benton, Louisiana 71006. Mr. Emmett Cope.
Brace School, 21705 Evergreen Road, Southfield, Michigan 48075. Ms. Barbara Mansfield.
Holdingford Public Schools, Holdingford, Minnesota. Mrs. Ruth Lackelt.
New Albany Public Schools, New Albany, Mississippi. Mr. Holace Morris.
Elementary Schools, Cape Giradeau, Missouri.
Friend Public School, Friend, Nebraska 68395. Mr. Rodney Bartells.
Highland-Goeffes Falls School, Goeffes Falls Road, Manchester, New Hampshire 03103. Miss Jeanette Saiger.

Mascenic Regional School, New Ipswich, New Hampshire 03071. Mrs. Doris Beane.
Mora School, State Department of Education, Sante Fe, New Mexico. Ms. Blanche Colle.
Marvin B. Smith Elementary School, 509 Huffman Mill Road, Burlington, North Carolina. Dr. Betty Bowman.
Hettinger High School, Hettinger, North Dakota. Mr. Gordon Reinke.
Athens High School, The Plains, Ohio 45701. Mr. Robert Stamp.
Tulsa Public Schools, P. O. Box 45208, Tulsa, Oklahoma 74145. Dr. Bruce Howell.
Ninety Six High School, Ninety Six, South Carolina 29666. Mr. J. S. Ritchie.
Brooking Public School, Brooking, South Dakota 57006. Mr. Paul Johnson.
Westside School Project, Sisseton Public Schools, Sisseton, South Dakota 57262. Mr. Pete Robenberg.
Dodson Elementary School, 4401 Changler Road, Hermitage, Tennessee 37076. Mr. Carl K. Ross.
Lynchburg City Schools, 11th and Court Street, Lynchburg, Virginia 24504. Dr. John A. Eberhart.
Oregon Middle School, Oregon, Wisconsin. Mr. Roland Cross.

Curriculum

Metropolitan Youth Education Center, Denver Public Schools, 414 14th Street, Denver, Colorado 80202. Mr. Robert Hirsch.
Widefield Public Schools, 701 Widefield Drive, Security, Colorado 80911. Mr. W. L. Stenson.
Mount Pleasant School District, Washington Street Extension and Marsh Road, Wilmington, Delaware 19809. Ms. Lucille K. Sherman.
Nova High School, 3600 S.W. 70th Ave., Fort Lauderdale, Florida 33314. Mr. John Arena.
Hawaii English Project, Department of Education, 1625 Wist Place, Honolulu, Hawaii 96822. Mrs. Grace Fujita.
Murray Road Annex, Newton High School, 35 Murray Road, West Newton, Massachusetts, 02165. Mr. Richard Mechem.
Hoover Elementary School, Carmen Community Schools, G2165 LaVelle Road, Flint, Michigan 48504. Mr. Dale Wolfe.
Mount Clemens Public Schools, Mt. Clemens, Michigan. Mr. William Harding.
McClure Senior High School, Ferguson-Florissant Public Schools, Florissant, Missouri 63135. Dr. Roger Bridenkamp.
Nashua High School, Nashua, Montana 59248. Mr. William Willarize.
Geneva Public Schools, 1011 0 Street, Geneva, Nebraska 86361. Mr. Larry Westerbuhr.
Department of Education, State of New Jersey, 225 W. State Street, P. O. Box 2019, Trenton, New Jersey 08625. Mr. Anthony E. Conte.
Williston High School, Williston, North Dakota. Mr. Leon Olson.
Judson Junior High School, 4512 Jones Road South East, Salem, Oregon 97302. Mr. Thomas B. Hornig.
Bellafante Area Secondary School, Bellafante, Pennsylvania.
Seneca High School, P. O. Box 917, Seneca, South Carolina 29678. Mr. Paul Dover.
Ponape Agriculture and Trade School, Ponape, Caroline Islands, Trust Territory of the Pacific 96941. Mr. Richard J. Becker.
Lander Valley High School, Lander, Wyoming. Mr. Jack King.

Differentiated Staffing

Ocean View Elementary School, 7972 Warner Avenue, Huntington Beach, California. Dr. Clarence Hall.
Temple City Unified School District, 9516 East Longden Avenue, Temple City, California 91780. Mr. Robert E. Lundgren.
Lincoln Elementary School, Staples, Minnesota. Mr. Richard Hegie.
Mary Harmon Weeks Elementary School, 47201 Indiana, Kansas City, Missouri 64130. Mr. Eugene Wolkey.
L. E. Berger Middle School, West Fargo, North Dakota. Mr. L. E. Berger.
Beaverton School District 48, 4855 S.W. Erickson Street, Beaverton, Oregon 97005. Mr. Harold V. Wik.

Early Childhood, Pre-School

Eldora Community Schools, Eldora, Iowa 50627. Mr. George J. Rinehart.
Springfield Avenue Community School, 447 18th Ave., Newark, New Jersey. Mr. Joseph J. McSweeney.
South Umpqua School District #19, P. O. Box 649, Myrtle Creek, Oregon 97457. Dealous L. Cox.

Individually Guided Education

Anniston Public Schools, P. O. Box 1500, Anniston, Alabama 36201. Dr. George Layton.
West Elementary School, Cullman, Alabama. Mr. Raymond Clark.
Meadowlane Elementary School, 709 Meadowland Drive, Phenix City, Alabama 36867. Mr. Louis E. Brummett.
Vance Elementary School, Vance, Alabama 35490.
Tempe School District #3, P. O. Box 27708, Tempe, Arizona 85281. Dr. John W. Simonds.
Whittier University Laboratory School, University of California, Berkeley, California 94700. Ms. Irish and Ms. Christianson.
Arevalos School, Fountain Valley School District, 9502 Velardo Drive, Huntington Beach, California. Dr. Edward W. Beaubier.
Patrick Henry Senior High School, San Diego City Schools, 4100 Normal Street, San Diego, California 92103. Dr. Jack Stone.
Altura Boulevard Elementary School, 1650 Altura Boulevard, Aurora, Colorado 80010. Mr. John Dale.
Chelteham Elementary School, 1580 Julian Street, Denver, Colorado 80204. Mrs. Virginia Hansen.
Green Gables Elementary School, 8701 West Woodward Drive, Denver, Colorado 80226. Dr. Charles Teal.
Bergen Elementary School, Evergreen, Colorado 80439. Mr. Lawrence Schrader.
Riffenburgh Elementary School, Poudre R-I, Fort Collins, Colorado. Mr. Robert Asmus.
Greeley Public Schools, 811 - 15th Street, Greeley, Colorado 80631. Mr. Arthur R. Partridge.
Clear Creek Elementary School, Idaho Springs, Colorado 80452. Mr. Earl Kennedy.
Clear Creek Secondary School, Idaho Springs Public Schools, Idaho Springs, Colorado 80452. Mr. R. Metzler.
Green Mountain Elementary School, 12250 West Kentucky Drive, Lakewood, Colorado 80228. Mr. William Boland.
Normandy Elementary School, 809 Quail Street, Lakewood, Colorado 80215. Mr. Carl R. Zerger.
Big Thompson Elementary School, 585 Big Thompson Road, Loveland, Colorado 80537.
Cedartown High School, Polk County Schools, Cedartown, Georgia 30125. Dr. Guy Taylor.
College Community School District, 401 - 76 Avenue S.W., Cedar Rapids, Iowa 52401. Mr. James A. Bayne.
Eagle Grove Community Schools, Eagle Grove, Iowa 50533. Mr. Allan Peters.
Linn-Mar Community Schools, North 10th Street, Marion, Iowa 52303. Dr. Le Roy L. Kruskop.
Pleasant Valley Elementary School, Pleasant Valley, Iowa 52767. Mr. Ed. D. Fauble.
Unified School District, Council Grove, Kansas 66846. Mr. Ronald Moore.
South High School, Salina, Kansas. Dr. Floyd Coppedge.
Shawnee Mission Northwest High School, Shawnee Mission, Kansas 66200. Dr. Merlin Ludwig.
Cumberland Elementary Schools, Cumberland, Maine. Mr. Reginald Dews.
Telstar Regional High School, Bethel, Maine 04217. Mr. Brian Flynn.
Amherst School District, Amherst, Massachusetts. Mr. Ronald Fitzgerald.
Learning Village, 541 Phelps Street, Kalamazoo, Michigan Dr. 1, Dr. Roger E. Ulrich.
Franklin Stevenson High School, Livonia Public Schools, 15125 Farmington Road, Livonia, Michigan 48154. Mr. Don Friedrich.
Robert J. Hesse Elementary School, 29800 Boewe, Warren, Michigan 48092. Mr. Patrich Brown.

Thomas Jefferson High School, Bloomington, Minnesota. Mr. Fred Atkinson.
Stonebridge Elementary School, Independent School District #834, 1018 South First Street, Stillwater, Minnesota 55082. Mr. Garld J. Smith.
Southview Elementary School, Waconia, Minnesota. Mr. James J. Kovaleski.
Camp Elementary School, Hattiesburg, Mississippi 39401. Dr. Sam Spinks.
Jackson Mississippi Schools, 662 South President Street, Jackson, Mississippi 39201. Dr. Brandon Sparkman.
Hickman High School, Columbia Public Schools, Columbia, Missouri 65201. Mr. Kenneth Clark.
North Kansas City High School, North Kansas City, Missouri. Dr. Robert Howe.
Horton Watkins High School, 1201 South Warson Road, St. Louis, Missouri 63124. Mr. Ed. Times.
Mountain View Elementary School, Great Falls, Montana. Dr. Harold Wennas.
Randolph Elementary School, 1204 South 37th, Lincoln, Nebraska 68510. Mr. Richard Althoff.
Archbishop Ryan High School, 5616 L. Street, Omaha, Nebraska 68117. Sister Pacis.
William E. Ferron Elementary School, 4200 Mountain View, Las Vegas, Nevada 89109. Mr. Jack Dailey.
C.V.T. Gilbert School, 2101 West Cartier Avenue, Las Vegas, Nevada. Dr. Edna Hinman.
Las Vegas Urban High School, 2839 South Burnham Street, Las Vegas, Nevada 89105. Mr. Gerald F. Hurt.
Jonathan M. Daniels School, Maple Avenue, Keene, New Hampshire 03431. Mr. Henry J. Grauque.
Pinecrest High School, Southern Pines, North Carolina 28387. Mr. J. R. Brendle.
Clara Barton Elementary School, 1417 Sixth Street South, Fargo, North Dakota 58102. Mr. Donovan C. Nelson.
Kelly School, Grand Forks, North Dakota. Mr. Jerry L. Abbott.
Red River High School, Grand Forks, North Dakota. Mr. Everett Knudsvig.
Butler Senior High School, 600 South Dixie Drive, Vandalia, Ohio 45377. Mr. B. P. Gibson.
Burbank Dep. District, Burbank, Oklahoma 74633. Mr. Mickey D. Bock.
Hood River Valley High School, Route 4, Box 270, Hood River, Oregon 97031. Mr. Charles S. Bowe.
Woodlawn Elementary School, 7200 N.E. 11th Avenue, Portland, Oregon 97211. Mr. Robert P. Selby.
Melville School, Portsmouth, Rhode Island. Mr. Richard Donnelly.
Samoana High School, Pago Pago, American Samoa. Aleni Ripine.
Douglas School District, Ellsworth Air Force Base, Rapid City, South Dakota 57706. Dr. Eldon E. Gran.
12th Street Elementary School, Taylor Independent School District, 113 W. 4th Street, Taylor, Texas 76574. Mr. Joe B. Scrivner.
Leo J. Muir Elementary School, Bountiful, Utah. Mr. Arnold Lund.
Tooele East Elementary School, 150 South 7th Street, Tooele, Utah 84074. Mr. James A. Gowans.
Henry S. Baird School, 539 Laverne Drive, Green Bay, Wisconsin 54311.
Southwest High School, 100 North Jefferson, Green Bay, Wisconsin 54305. Mr. Jerome McCormick.
Madison Public Schools, 545 West Dayton Street, Madison, Wisconsin 53703. Mr. Douglas Ritchie.

Open Plan School

Butterfield Trail Elementary School, Fayetteville, Arkansas 72701. Mr. Dean May.
Zion Heights Junior High School, North York, Canada.
Lowndes County Public School System, Valdosta, Georgia 31601.
Zackary Lane Elementary School, Plymouth, Minnesota. Mr. William Forsberg.
Graham School, Ferguson-Florissant School District, 1150 Graham Road, Florissant, Missouri 63135. Mr. Paul R. Bueneman.
Daley Elementary School, 411 Daley Avenue, Hamilton, Montana 59840.
Ord Public Schools, Ord, Nebraska. Dr. William Gagan.
Paul A. Smith Elementary School, Lawndale Avenue, Franklin, New Hampshire 03235. Mr. Robert Ross.
East Rochester Elementary School, East Rochester, New Hampshire. Mr. Alfred W. Thomas.

Henryette Public Schools, Henryette, Oklahoma 74437. Dr. Raymond Cox.
Temple Elementary School, Temple, Texas.
The Prospect School, North Bennington, Vermont. Mrs. Marian Taylor.
Jackson-Via School, Harris Road, Charlottesville, Virginia 22903. S. Scott Hamrick.
West Valley Public Schools, Route 4, Box 307, Yakima, Washington 98902. Dr. Walter C. Seiler.
Andrew Jackson Junior High School, 5445 Big Tyler Road, Charleston, West Virginia 25312. Mr. John Santrock.
Edison Junior High School, Janesville, Wisconsin.

Organizational Techniques

Beaverhaven and Oak Park Middle Schools, Decatur City Schools, 210 Wilson Street, N.E., Decatur, Alabama 35601. Mr. Robert Bumpus.
Lamar County Secondary Schools, P. O. Box 469, Vernon, Alabama 35592.
Ontario High School, Francis Street, Ontario, California 91761. Mr. James Randles.
Bell Junior High School, 1001 Ulysses Street, Golden, Colorado 80401. Mr. George Carnie.
Kullerstrand Elementary Schools, Wheatridge, Colorado 80033. Mr. Kenneth R. Vendena.
Lowndes County Public School System, Valdosta, Georgia 31601.
Eldora Community Schools, Eldora, Iowa 50627. Mr. George J. Rinehart.
Keokuk Junior High School, Keokuk, Iowa. Mr. Robert Leland.
Mason City Community School District, Mason City, Iowa. Mr. Rod Bickert.
Conkwright Middle School, Winchester, Kentucky 40391. Mr. Donald W. Pace.
Baltimore City Public Schools, 3 East 25th Street, Baltimore, Maryland 21218. Dr. Vernon Vevrirada.
Walt Whitman High School, Bethesda, Maryland. Mrs. Nancy Hoon.
Okemos High School, 4000 North Okemos Road, Okemos, Michigan. Mr. William Dean.
Dover High School, Durham Road, Dover, New Hampshire 03820. Mr. C. Harvey Knipp.
Columbia High School, South Orange-Maplewood District, South Orange, New Jersey 07079. Dr. Herbert McDavit.
Maplewood Junior High School, South Orange, New Jersey 07079.
Parkway High School, Philadelphia, Pennsylvania. Mr. Leonard B. Finkelstein.
Shelbourne Middle School, Shelbourne, Vermont. Dr. John Winton.
Franklin Junior High School, Janesville, Wisconsin.
Marshall Junior High School, Janesville, Wisconsin.

Scheduling

Brookurst Junior High Schools, Anaheim, California 92801.
Mitchell Senior High School, 1205 Patter Drive, Colorado Springs, Colorado 80909. Mr. Ronald L. Walden.
Skyline High School, 150 N. Water Street, Idaho Falls, Idaho 83401. Dr. Jay Casper.
Evanston Township High School, Evanston, Illinois. Mrs. Wanda Mitchell.
Burris Laboratory School, Ball State University, Muncie, Indiana 43706. Dr. Kenneth Foster.
Eagle Grove Community Schools, Eagle Grove, Iowa 50533. Mr. Allan Peters.
Keokuk Junior High School, Keokuk, Iowa. Mr. Robert Leland.
Mason City Community School District, Mason City, Iowa. Mr. Rod Bickert.
Columbus High School, 3231 West Ninth Street, Waterloo, Iowa 50702. Reverend Father Walter Brunkan.
Eisenhower Senior High School, Hopkins, Minnesota. Mr. Don Coppins.
Hopkins Senior High School, Hopkins, Minnesota. Mr. Dennis Roof.
Oak-Land Junior High School, Stillwater, Minnesota. Mr. Kenneth LaCroix.
Oak Park High School, North Kansas City Public Schools, North Kansas City, Missouri. Dr. Dan Kahler.
Briarcliff High School, Briarcliff Manor, New York 10510. Mr. Gardiner Dumran.
Alton U. Farnsworth Middle School, Guilderland Central Schools, State Farm Road, Guilderland, New York 12084. Dr. Kenneth Kimball.
Pleasantville Middle School, Pleasantville, New York. Dr. Leighton Wilklow.
Bend High School, Bend, Oregon. Mr. Don Brown.

Marshall High School, 3905 S.E. 91st Avenue, Portland, Oregon 97266. Dr. Gaynor Petrequin.
Parkrose Heights Junior High, 12456 N.E. Brazer Street, Portland, Oregon 97230. Mr. Edwin E. Goodling.
John Marshall High School, 1300 Wheeling Avenue, Glendale, West Virginia 26038.
Craig Senior High School, Janesville, Wisconsin.
George S. Parker High School, Janesville, Wisconsin.

Special Education

Steamboat Springs Public Schools, P. O. Box 1234, Steamboat Springs, Colorado 80477. Mr. Donald J. Sanders.
Marshalton-McKean School District, 1703 School Lane, Wilmington, Delaware 19808. Mr. Frederick Boyer.
Hillsborough County Public Schools, 1105 Bermuda Boulevard, Tampa, Florida 33605. Ms. Joanne F. Rocco.
DeKalb County Schools, 385 Glendale Road, Scottdale, Georgia 30079. Jeptha V. Greer.
Little Harbour School, Portsmouth, New Hampshire.

Teacher-Education—Inservice Education

Claremont Graduate School of Education, Claremont, California 91711. Dr. Carolyn L. Ellner.
Palm Beach County School District, P. O. Box 2469, West Palm Beach, Florida 33402. Mr. John C. Thurber.

Technology and Media

Etowah County Board of Education, Courthouse, Gadsden, Alabama 35901. Mr. C. C. Davis.
Myers Demonstration Library, Box 4040, 5000 E. Andrew, Tucson, Arizona 85717. Mrs. Murvise Odom.
Burris Laboratory School, Ball State University, Muncie, Indiana 47306. Dr. Kenneth Foster.
South Orange Junior High School, 219 South Orange Street, South Orange, New Jersey 07079. Mr. Shelton E. Goble.
Oklahoma City Public Schools, 900 North Klein, Oklahoma City, Oklahoma 73106. Dr. Mervel S. Lunn.

Year-Round Schools

Vann W. Ferguson School, Hawaiian Gardens, California.
Baltimore City Public Schools, 3 East 25th St., Baltimore, Maryland 21218. Dr. Vernon Vevrirada.

Selected References

California State Department of Education, "The California Pace." Sacramento; 1970, 324 pp. (mimeographed).

Education U.S.A. Special Report, "Individualization in Schools—The Challenge And The Options," Washington, D. C.: The National School Public Relations Association, 1971, 64 pp.

Featherstone, Joseph, *Schools Where Children Learn,* New York: Liveright, 1971, 180 pp.

Macbeth, Edwin W., "When The Walls Come Tumbling Down," "An Open Plan Encourages an Open Program," and "No Doubt What They Had in Mind," *School Management,* Volume 15, Number 8, August, 1971, pp. 8-17.

Maine Department of Education, Title III Office, "Teaching Is For Kids," Augusta, Maine, 1970, 44 pp. (mimeographed).

Minnesota Department of Education, "Listing of Experimental Programs Now in Operation in Minnesota Public Schools," St. Paul, November 1970, 9 pp. (mimeographed).

Minnesota School Facilities Council, "Individualized Instruction, The Year Round School, Education for the 70's," Report of Conference, September 30 - October 2, 1970. Minneapolis (2650 Stinson Boulevard): 1970, 189 pp.

National Education Association "The Teacher and His Staff: Selected Demonstration Centers, Washington, D. C., NEA, 1967, 143 pp.

"Open-Space Schools Project Bulletin," School Planning Laboratory, School of Education, Stanford University, Number 1, March, 1970.

Resnik, Henry S., "The Open Classroom," *Today's Education,* December, 1971, p. 16.

Shofstall, W. P., "Arizona ESEA Title III Pacesetters," Phoenix, Arizona: Department of Education, 1971-72, 52 pp. (mimeographed).

U. S. Department of Health, Education, and Welfare, Bureau of Educational Personnel Development, Office of Education, *How Teachers Make a Difference,* Washington, U. S. Government Printing Office, 1971, 166 pp.